Correct Thinking Saves Marriage

Discovering the Way Forward When the "I's" Have It

by Dr. Peter Joseph

DORRANCE
PUBLISHING CO
EST. 1920
PITTSBURGH, PENNSYLVANIA 15235

The contents of this work, including, but not limited to, the accuracy of events, people, and places depicted; opinions expressed; permission to use previously published materials included; and any advice given or actions advocated are solely the responsibility of the author, who assumes all liability for said work and indemnifies the publisher against any claims stemming from publication of the work.

All Rights Reserved
Copyright © 2022 by Dr. Peter Joseph

No part of this book may be reproduced or transmitted, downloaded, distributed, reverse engineered, or stored in or introduced into any information storage and retrieval system, in any form or by any means, including photocopying and recording, whether electronic or mechanical, now known or hereinafter invented without permission in writing from the publisher.

Dorrance Publishing Co
585 Alpha Drive
Pittsburgh, PA 15238
Visit our website at *www.dorrancebookstore.com*

ISBN: 978-1-6376-4246-7
eISBN: 978-1-6376-4562-8

Praise for Correct Thinking Saves Marriage

In this little book, Dr. Joseph helps solve a big problem. While neither of the greatest two commandments—love God; love others—highlights "I," our culture has put the self at the center of the world. This sinful approach that is old as humanity shows up in our marriages. In a time when the very definition of marriage is under attack, Dr. Joseph uses the Bible, his education, and ministry experience to help couples overcome the selfishness that infects the most intimate relationship outside of our relationship with God. The questions he asks at the end of each chapter are both diagnostic and prescriptive for the health of a marriage—just what the doctor ordered! These questions should be built into pre-marital counseling as well as marriage retreats to help strengthen marriages plagued with "I."

—Danny R. Bowen, PhD, Adjunct
Professor, South Western Baptist Theological Seminary.

Incorrect thinking has invaded our marriages. The basic incorrect idea is that a good marriage consists of two people. Author Peter Joseph says that good marriage actually involves three persons—the third one being God. Only by following God's design for marriage can two sin-inclined partners escape their own self-interests to faithfully love each other and glorify God through their marriage. Common self-interests are cleverly identified by chapter titles, each title consisting of an obviously selfish statement such as, "I don't care what you think," "I am not the problem," "I don't feel like I am in love anymore." Each chapter sets about to disprove the statement. Even if a marriage partner may not say these words aloud, the way they behave may clearly demonstrate the thoughts.

The book would function well in small group setting. Discussion questions provided at the end of each chapter will expand the value of the book as people contribute ideas from their unique perspective.

—Jane Thayer, PhD, Professor, Andrews University
Author *of Strategies for Transformational Learning: How to teach for Discipleship*

Dr. Peter Joseph, in this notable and enlightening book *CORRECT THINKING SAVES MARRIAGE: Discovering the way forward when the "I's" have it*, has delivered a remarkable contribution for the improvement of marriages and family relationships. His careful and erudite treatment of the subject will make this book a treasure to readers at any stage of family life—pre-marriage, courtship, or marriage.

The concept of right thinking runs throughout the book; and Dr. Joseph skillfully articulates deleterious effects of a self-centered focus in our interpersonal relationships. The spiritual and biblical underpinnings in this work greatly enhance its value. Many of the significant challenges faced in family relationships are explored and efficiently handled.

If those who are preparing for marriage could be exposed to the principles Dr. Joseph outlines between these pages, they will be put on a path to success and happiness in their marriages. Those who are already married will discover several areas where they can make a failing marriage succeed, and a good marriage even better.

The book is made even more pragmatic and useful by the discussion questions at the end of each chapter. It will be most welcomed by small groups for studying together. We have been engaged in family-life education for more than forty years, in Inter- American Division of Seventh-day Adventists and the Caribbean Union; and this book we would readily recommend to young people preparing for marriage, to those who wish to improve their marriages, and also to church groups.

We pray that this book, *Correct Thinking Saves Marriage: Discovering the way forward when the "I's have it*, will get the circulation it deserves.

—Pastor Jansen Trotman, DD, MA, CFLE, CC
Gloria Trotman, PhD, MA, CFLE, CC

The book *Correct Thinking Saves Marriage* serves as a powerful resource to strengthen the institution of marriage, a founding pillar of society. It posits the notion of appropriate and responsible thinking which is made possible by the Originator of Family, God Himself. As the information shared is beneficial to married couples and those preparing for marriage, I endorse this well-researched work that is supported with biblical references and cites well-known authorities on marriage and the family. Additionally, each chapter ends with discussion questions, which are useful for marital counseling and marriage seminars and retreats. Overall, the book is a welcomed tool in the fight against incidents of divorce and for fortifying families, and by extension, the society.

—Leonard A. Johnson, DMin, CMG, JP
EXECUTIVE SECRETARY
Inter- American Division of Seventh-day Adventists

For the last fifteen years I have had the distinct pleasure of knowing Dr. Joseph as both a graduate student and pastor. He exemplifies a humble, open and eager mind as a servant leader, as well as a strong work ethic that I have been privy to as an instructional leader, co-laborer and observer. He is a multi-talented man whose spiritual gifts include a burning drive to foster God endowed marriages. As such, I strongly endorse this book for individuals interested in improving their own marriages as well as for those who have spiritual leadership gifts to use in leading others into Christ-centered marriages. Having undertaken presentations with Dr. Joseph, I know he provides biblical foundations and solutions for marital conflict. This is a driving passion of his. He recognizes that marriages are undertaken with honorable and loving intentions, but they turn into home-based dictatorships. He refers to such as the tyrannous actions caused largely by flaws in our human nature, specifically that people think one way but act another. As a counter to this, readers can expect to find strategies and helps for active listening, mutual reflection, attitude adjustment, working to outcome, valuing, various perspectives, recognizing the enemy within, as well as other finely tuned approaches to improving the path to a Spirit-led marriage. I know Dr. Joseph's work will make a positive difference in the lives of all who read and prayerfully apply the concepts and advice.

—Dr. Ray Ostrander, PhD
Professor of Teaching, Learning and Curriculum
Andrews University

The book is a must read for those already married and those who may be contemplating entering a marital relationship. Dr. Peter Joseph shows what many seem not to understand—that relationships are affected more by pattern of thinking of those in the relationship than by any other single factor. Sow a thought then reap a destiny. He also applied the incontestable truth that there is a visible unseen warfare that is raging in minds and relationships. I gladly recommend this book to all who engage in human interactions.

—James Daniel, PhD (Edu)
Vice President
General Conference, Inter-American Division of Seventh-day Adventists

I congratulate my friend and ministerial colleague Dr. Peter Joseph for the profoundly exciting and refreshing exposition on marriage in this book, *Correct Thinking Saves Marriage: Discovering the way forward when the "I's" have it.*

This book could not have been written at a more critical moment. It is coming at a time when families are in crisis and the institution of marriage is under brutal attack, and when the world is suffering from the vicious, deadly coronavirus pandemic which has intensified the pressure for the survival of many marriages.

Dr. Peter Joseph has brought his many years of experience as a pastor, evangelist, marriage officer, and marriage counsellor to bear on the writing of this book. I am impressed with its theological depth and soundness, and its practical application.

This book makes for easy, relaxing reading. While offering wise counsel and encouragement, it also serves to inspire confidence and hope in the hearts of married couples and other readers at a time when we need them most.

—Peter Kerr, DD, MA
President
Atlantic Caribbean Union of Seventh-day Adventists

In a time when the very definition of marriage is under attack, Dr. Joseph uses the Bible, his education and ministry experience to help couples overcome the selfishness that infects the most intimate relationship outside of our relationship with God. The questions he asked at the end of each chapter are both diagnostic and prescriptive for the health of marriage—just what the doctor ordered! These questions should be built into premarital counseling as well as marriage retreats to help strengthen marriages plagued with "I."

—Danny R. Bowen, PhD, Adjunct
Professor, South Western Baptist Theological Seminary

Dr. Joseph skillfully articulates deleterious effects of self-centered focus in our interpersonal relationships. The spiritual and biblical underpinnings in this work greatly enhance its value. Many of the significant challenges faced in family relationships are explored and efficiently handled.

—Pastor Jansen Trotman, DD, MA, CFLE, CC
Gloria Trotman, PhD, MA, CFLE, CC

Common self-interests are cleverly identified by the chapter titles, each title consisting of an obviously selfish statement such as, "I don't care what you think," "I am not the problem," "I don't feel like I am in love anymore." Each chapter sets about to disprove the statement. Even if a marriage partner may not say these words aloud, the way they behave may clearly demonstrate their thoughts. This book would function well in small group setting. Discussion questions provided at the end of each chapter will expand the value of the book as people contribute ideas from their unique perspectives.

—Jane Thayer, PhD
Professor, Andrews University
Author of *Strategies for Transformational Learning:
How to teach for Discipleship*

The book *Correct Thinking Saves Marriage* serves as a powerful resource to strengthen the institution of marriage, a founding pillar of society.
—Leonard A. Johnson, DMin, CMG, JP, EXECUTIVE SECRETARY
Inter- American Division of Seventh-day Adventists

Dr. Joseph recognizes that marriages are undertaken with honorable and loving intentions, but they turn into home-based dictatorships. He refers to such as the tyrannous actions caused largely by flaws in our human nature, specifically that people think one way and act another. As a counter to this, readers can expect to find strategies and helps for active listening, mutual reflection, attitude adjustment, working to outcome, valuing various perspectives, recognizing the enemy within, as well as other finely tuned approaches to improving the path to Spirit-led marriages.
—Dr. Ray Ostrander, PhD
Professor of Teaching, Learning and Curriculum, Andrews University

Dr. Peter Joseph has brought his many years of experience as a pastor, evangelist, marriage officer and marriage counselor to bear on writing this book. I am impressed with the theological soundness and practical application.
—Peter Kerr, DD, MA
President, Atlantic Caribbean Union of Seventh-day Adventist

A most profound and practical resource that gets to the root of what's wrong with many marriages and provides timeless biblical strategies that contribute to happy and lasting marriages in an excellent way.
—Howard Simon MA, CFLE
District Pastor, North Caribbean Conference of Seventh- day Adventist

This book is a must read for those already married and those who may be contemplating entering a marital relationship. Dr. Peter Joseph shows what many seem not to understand—that relationships are affected more by pattern of thinking of those in the relationship than by any other single factor.

—James Daniel, PhD (Edu.)
Vice President
General Conference, Inter-American Division of Seventh-day Adventists

Peter Joseph (DEd Min, The Southern Baptist Theological Seminary) is a family education, leadership, discipleship and evangelism consultant, author, and speaker living in Nassau, Bahamas, with his wife Michelle.

CONTENTS

ACKNOWLEDGMENTS

I have seen God use good marriages to sanctify spouses and enlighten society with Judeo-Christian values. But I have also seen bad marriages that tend to deliver abuse, pain, misery, and hopelessness to spouses and moral decay to society. As a son of separated parents, I know too well the negative effects of bad marriages. One thing that I have become acutely aware of as a husband is the supernatural battle that takes place in marriages. Once I understood that revelation, then I ceased to become the arbiter of my own marriage and humbly submit to the God who reveals himself in Holy Scripture for guidance in the way I think and live. In response to marital events, I think not in self-improvement terms but for the glory of God. My marriage is to glorify God. In this way, spouses save themselves from the human weaknesses of one another.

Writing a book is not a solitary journey. The many team members of WINNING YOUR MARRIAGE CONFERENCE, who often interact with me on salient ideas of marital satisfaction, made this book possible. The variety of speakers, like Pastor Howard Simon, Dr. Raymond Ostrander, Dr. Pansy Hamilton Brown, Dr. Antoinette Darling, Mrs. Patrice Gordon, Pastor Larry Green, Pastor Barrington Brennen, Jacqueline Gibson, Pastor Asha Dane Duncan, Pastor Levi Johnson, Dr. Joseph Evans, and Dr. Paul and Mrs. Joan Scavella finetuned ideas in presentations that made their way in this resource. The unstinting support of my mother-in-law, Ruth McKinney, and quiet motivation from my sons Newton and Edmund are part of the reason why we are here gladly.

Michelle, my wife, remains the best wife I know. Thank you for being there in both my weakness and strength as we bear witness to the glory of God. Your wisdom in uncertainty and courage in lean times make God looks good on you. I dedicate this book to you.

INTRODUCTION

C hristian marriages should embody civilization's highest aspirations. In fact, marriages represent doors of opportunity for an orderly and productive family of procreation, and the wellbeing of communities and societies. Thus, every generation should see the lasting benefit of preparing the next generation for marriage. However, marriage today can evoke images of conflict, rage, misunderstanding, and abuse. So, while marriage may be looked upon with hope, a gripping fear exists as worry, frustration, and distress continue to be part and parcel of what should be the sacred precincts of marital bliss. The ambivalence about marriage is readily evident in the daily lives of mates, and the animated public discourses.

We love our marriage. Yet, many couples wrestle with a troubling reality—when they desire good, evil is present. Consequently, mates often seek therapeutic help that may not get to the root of the problem. The condition is symptomatic of a spiritual crisis. "Ultimately, we human beings, whether we realize it or not, are involved in a cosmic spiritual conflict that pits God against Satan, with marriage and family serving as a key arena in which spiritual and cultural battles are fought."[1]

An exploration of the functions of marriage may be helpful. For instance, when one examines intimate relationships, economic cooperation and consumption,

---

[1] Andreas J. Kostenberger with David W. Jones, *God, Marriage and Family: Rebuilding the Biblical Foundation* (Wheaton, IL: CROSSWAY, 2010), 15. The replacement of Judeo-Christian values by values of self-fulfillment and human rights are identified with a cultural crisis. This is symptomatic of a spiritual crisis. Therefore, the solution must be spiritual.

reproduction and socialization, and assignment of social roles and individual status, he may expose inequalities in areas of responsibilities, which may be the contributing factors for dysfunctions. However, the inequalities found in the functions of marriage are only symptomatic of the couple's spiritual condition. Therefore, the functions should not be addressed in isolation.

The epicenter of the spiritual crisis is not in the functions of marriage but the spouses themselves. The thoughts of couples have been estranged from God's thoughts. Therefore, too many couples are not thinking from a position of faith. Essentially, a position of faith has to do with a relationship with God, where the mind of God informs what and how a couple thinks about marriage. When the mind of God informs the minds of couples, then correct thinking ensues. If couples would think correctly, there would be correct responses to events in marriage, which infuse radiant energy in the marriage.

Marriage reflects the mind of the Creator. Therefore, couples should interpret marriage in light of a relationship with God and God's revelation. In other words, couples' derivative knowledge of marriage should come from the mind of God. God has constituted a meaningful and personal system of thought in the Bible. There resides a tree of life for correct thinking. However, in many ways, marriage today faces what Harry Blamires exclaimed, "There is no longer a Christian mind."[2] This condition has enormous consequences for Christian marriage because the longevity of marriage that glorifies God requires a Christian mind. Further, any criteria for marital life that reflect non-Christian or secular values will not bring glory to God and could only contribute to the relentless collapse of marriages. Essentially, incorrect thinking is the reason why the tyrannous "I's" have colonized many marriages. In other words, the **"I's" have it**. The colonization continues unabated as self-fulfillment has effectively replaced surrender and glorifying God.

Correct thinking saves marriages because correct thinking includes surrender and brings glory to God. The first couple, Adam and Eve, had an opportunity to think correctly and bring glory to God and, thus, avert the misery of the Fall, but they opted for incorrect thinking. Their marriage and successive marriages have paid an expensive price (Genesis 3–6). Every marriage faces situations where couples would have to think correctly to protect the marriage from debilitating scars. "We human beings were created

---

[2] Harry Blamires, *The Christian Mind: How Should A Christian Think?* (Ann Arbor, MI: Servant Books, 1978), 3.

to display God's character in the way we think, in what we desire and how we act."[3] The very character of God is at stake in the way couples think and respond to events in marriage. Moreover, marriage is an area of greatest return and therefore should be prioritized for correct thinking. "By focusing our attention on the areas of greatest return, we reap the greatest reward."[4] In order to understand the significance of correct thinking, consider the result of incorrect thinking in the first marriage.

The anatomy of incorrect thinking is inescapably emblazoned in the marital experience of the first pair. Eve failed to reason from a standpoint of faith. Marriage requires complete faith and trust in God. In fact, Satan's first line of attack is to assault faith in God. Notice Satan's assault on faith. He said to Eve, "Did God really say you must not eat from any tree in the garden?" (Genesis 3:1) Eve responded, "We may eat fruit from the trees in the garden, But God did say 'you must not eat from the tree that is in the middle of the garden, and you must not touch it or you will die'" (Genesis 3:2–3). Satan continued, "You will not surely die. For God knows that when you eat of it your eyes will be opened and you will be like God, knowing good and evil" (Genesis 3:4–5). Interestingly, Eve did not quote God's word correctly. God said, "You are free to eat from any tree of the garden, but you must not eat from the tree of the knowledge of good and evil, for when you eat of it you will surely die" (Genesis 2:16–17). Eve added "touch" to what God said and subtracted "surely" from God's explicit command. Even when Satan assaulted faith by saying "you shall not surely die"—a complete negation of what God said— Eve continued to engage Satan and doubted the word of God.

It appears that Eve did not take God's word with the degree of seriousness and earnestness. Even though Eve was made in the image of God, yet when Satan told her that she shall be as God by eating from the forbidden tree, she succumbed to self-fulfillment (Genesis 3:6). At that time the "I's" had it. Self-fulfillment is the foundation of incorrect thinking. Her husband, Adam, joined her. The marriage endured frustration, guilt, blame, shame, and pain. They did not think from a position of faith in God.

---

[3] Jeremy Pierre & Deepak Reju, *The Pastor and Counseling: The Basics of Shepherding Members in Need* (Wheaton, IL: CROSSWAY, 2015), 219.

[4] John C. Maxwell, *Thinking For A Change: 11 Ways Highly Successful People Approach Life and Work* (Center Street; 1st Edition, 2005), 300 Kindle eBook.

Correct thinking saves marriage. Yet, in many marriages, the poignant replay of Adam and Eve's incorrect thinking is demonstrable at an alarming level among couples. This book represents an attempt to identify incorrect thinking in marriages and explore correct thinking through the lens of the Bible. While the Bible will be relied upon, extra-biblical resources will reinforce the claims of scripture. This book does not engage in hypothesis testing but simply presents the claims of scripture, along with extra-biblical material to the marital context. The lack of correct thinking among so many Christian married couples has led to this book. For over twenty-five years, I have seen the deficiency in the matter of correct thinking in marriages. I write this book because I love marriage. However, I also write this book because of the anticipation that those who read this book will save marriages from the tyrannous "I's."

ABOUT THIS BOOK

Chapter one begins by posing a key question that every married person should ask. The answer to that question indicates a tendency to incorrect thinking or correct thinking. The question is designed to identify self-interest or a God-ward faith. Chapter two examines the work of the enemy within. It also exposes the tendency of spouses to enable addictive behaviors. Chapter three focuses on defaulting on listening as a service owed to each other, and the gender difference in the service rendered. Chapter four elaborates on working as a team to solve problems, and the primacy of closeness to avoid becoming "little gods." Chapter five explores the power of forgiveness to open the door to a bright future. It shows that the motive to be a blessing instead of searching for personal freedom result in forgiveness being more effective and long lasting. Chapter six zeros in on self-righteousness and shows how a Gospel attitude could replace self-righteous habits. Chapter seven addresses boundaries and the primacy of God to meet our ultimate need for boundaries. Chapter eight identifies the unmoored tongue as part of climate change in marriage that has the capacity to burn the marriage down to the ground. Chapter nine exposes the love affair with deficit spending and the appropriate financial disciplines to eliminate debt and credit buying. Chapter ten explains how to continue to love when "feelings of love" wane. Chapter eleven illuminates spiritual warfare in the arena of marriage. It identifies a strategy of prayer as the most effective weapon against evil forces.

We are not arbiters of our own marriages, as some of us may think. We dare not exist independent of God if we desire to resist the colonization of our marriages by the **tyrannous "I's."** We owe the beginning and continuation of our marriage to God. This reliance on God comes with the responsibility to think correctly.

I hope that presentations of the contents will resource spouses with practical and intellectual tools to think correctly. Given that I strongly believe that every generation should equip the next generation for marriage, I hope that this resource would equip the unmarried as well. Lastly, professionals who engage in teaching, preaching, pastoring, and Biblical counseling could use this resource as a means of equipping the next generation.

CHAPTER ONE

꙰

The tryrannous "I am having it my way."

Asking permission is critical, but so is the ability to hear a no or not now with grace. —Gary Smalley

Here is the critical question everyone in a marital relationship with another human being should ask[5]: is there someone outside of me—the infinite, personal but triune, transcendent but immanent, sovereign, omniscient, and good God—that I must take into account?[6] How one answers the question predisposes him or her to the tendency of correct thinking or incorrect thinking.

If the answer is no, the person is prone to have selfish, self-centered, narcissistic, and naturalistic ideas. Such is the stuff of incorrect thinking. A scene in the Gospel According to Matthew exposes the germ of incorrect thinking. After Jesus predicted his sacrificial death on a cross, Peter was

---

[5] James Emory White writes, "There is then a great divide when it comes to how we approach the act of thinking... Yet as broad as the divide may be, the essence of the chasm is simple: there is either something outside of ourselves that we must take into account or there is not." James Emory White, *A Mind For God* (Downers Grove IL: InterVarsity Press Books, 2006), 21.

[6] James W. Sire, *The Universe Next Door: A Basic Worldview Catalog* (Downers Grove, IL: InterVarsity Press, 1976), 26–28. God is infinite means he is primary and the source of everything. God is personal means he thinks and acts. Also human beings can know him in a personal and loving way and not simply that he exists. To be transcendent and immanent means God is beyond us and yet with us all at the same time. God is good in that he is holy and loving. Yet he sets the standard that people should live by.

1

dissatisfied. "Peter took him aside and began to rebuke him. 'Never Lord!' he said. 'This will never happen to you!' Jesus turned and said to Peter, 'Get behind me Satan! You are a stumbling block to me; you do not have in mind the things of God, but the things of men'" (Matt. 16:22–23). Notice, to have in mind the things of men is sinful, naturalistic, and selfish.

If the answer is yes, that we must take into account someone outside of us in our marital relationship, then the person tends to have other-centered and God-ward ideas in mind. Thus, the couple has the things of God in mind. This is the stuff of correct thinking. Correct thinking comes from bringing the things of God to bear on how one thinks about her marriage. When one acknowledges accountability to God, the ideas of God or the things of God tend to occupy the mind.

Essentially, to have the things of God in mind is to have a Christian mind. A Christian mind is needed for other-centeredness, faith, and spiritual intentions.

> The Christian mind is a mind that operates under the belief that there is something outside of ourselves that we must take into account. There is a God, as Francis Schaeffer said, who is not only there but is not silent. Thinking in light of God's existence and his self-revelation is what it means to have a Christian mind. It is seeing the world in light of faith.[7]

So, correct thinking requires that the mind be occupied with God—revelation in Jesus Christ, the Holy Spirit, and Scripture. The occupation of the mind with God is of great importance because the most important person in a relationship between a husband and wife is God. He provides the intellectual and spiritual resource needed to respond to events and each other with dignity, respect, and integrity. In fact, having the things of God in mind counters the sense of entitlement and points each person to a path of sacrifice and disciplined responses (Matt. 16:24).

What People Bring to Relationships

People bring what they have in mind to relationships—be it with God or human beings (Isaiah 14:12–14). What a person has in his mind has implications for relationships. For instance, the record of the Fall of Lucifer

---

[7] James Emery White, *A Mind For God* (Downers Grove IL: InterVarsity Press, Books, 2006), 21

indicates that he brought, mysteriously, a ton of negative energy and incorrect thinking to his relationship with God. Isaiah writes about the enigma. He says,

> How you have fallen from heaven, O morning star, son of the dawn! You have been cast down to the earth, you who once laid low the nations! You said in your heart, "I will ascend to heaven; I will raise my throne above the stars of God; I will sit enthroned on the mount of assembly, on the uttermost height of the sacred mountain. I will ascend above the tops of the clouds, I will be like the Most High" (Isaiah 14: 12–14).

The self-centeredness is alarming and appalling. Why is he behaving that way to a loving God? Incorrect thinking! He was obsessed with the notion of being God and saw his Creator as standing in the way of his goal (2 Samuel 15:1–4). The selfishness, self-centeredness, and narcissism are readily evident. For him, it was all about self-fulfillment.

The mystery of Lucifer's behavior is borne out in the revelation that God created him perfect in beauty and nature. Ezekiel points out, "You were blameless in your ways from the day you were created till wickedness was found in you" (Ezekiel 28:15). However, an internal tension of ideas—my way or God's way—soon resulted in a full-blown war in heaven and the expulsion of Lucifer and his minions. In graphic portrayal of a battle between two supernatural beings, John writes,

> And there was war in heaven. Michael and his angels fought against the Dragon, and the Dragon and his angels fought back. But he was not strong enough and they lost their place in heaven. The great Dragon was hurled down—that ancient serpent called the devil and Satan who leads the whole world astray. He was hurled to the earth and his angels with him (Revelation 12:7–9).

For Lucifer, it was all about self-fulfillment.

Incorrect thinking, which led to the rebellion, infected the first couple in the paradise of God. In crafty deception, Satan led the human race astray from

God and correct thinking. Bear in mind that the progenitors of the race, Adam and Eve, were created perfect.[8] Moses records the narrative of the fall of the first couple and the emergence of incorrect thinking in marital relationship.

> "Now the serpent was more crafty than any of the wild animals the Lord God had made. He said to the woman, Did God really say you must not to eat from any tree of the garden?... For God knows when you eat of it your eyes will be opened, and you will be like God, knowing good and evil. When the woman saw that the fruit of the tree was good for food and pleasing to the eye, and also desirable for gaining wisdom, she too some and ate it. She also gave some to her husband, who was with her, and he ate it (Genesis 3: 1–7).

Their relationship with God became soiled as they began to look out for their personal interests. They abandoned the relationship and proceeded to protect themselves from God. Genesis 3:8 says, "Then the man and his wife heard the sound of the Lord God as he was walking in the garden in the cool of the day and they hid from the Lord God among the trees." Looking out for one's self instead of the relationship became the *modus operandi* for successive generations (Romans 1:21).

In fact, when God called the man to account, he blamed his wife for the choice he made to rebel against the Creator. Similarly, when Eve was called into account, she blamed the serpent.[9] No one took responsibility for the fallen condition. They both brought what they had in mind to their relationship with each other. After a perfect start of their relationship, they turned on one another.[10] We often turn on one another after we revolt against God. Tragically, many a couple often turns on one another after covenanting to stay together for better for worse, for richer or poorer, in sickness and in health. The relational squabble began in paradise, which no subsequent relationship could escape.

Every relationship faces the possibility of fights over personality, words, ideas and ideology to the detriment of the relationship. The Genesis narrative

---

[8] Genesis 1: 31.

[9] Genesis 3:9–13.

[10] Genesis 2:18–25.

is a constant reminder that in any relationship, our minds are influenced either by God—His Revelation in Jesus Christ, the Holy Spirit, and Scripture—or Satan and his sophistries. "Satan's work is to influence people in such a way that the true function of creation is brought to ruination."[11] In like manner, Satan influences couples with a determined effort to ruin the true function of marriage. As such, he wants couples, in their minds, to move away from faith in God.

Purposefully, marriage presents daily opportunities to examine one's self whether he or she is in the faith. Paul writes in 2 Corinthians 5:13, "Examine yourself to see whether you are in the faith: test your selves. Do you not realize that Christ Jesus is in you—unless of course, you fail the test?" Webber is helpful when he writes, "In their Christian existence believers are ruled only by God's Word, which instruct them in all matters pertaining to their spiritual existence."[12] Marriage is one of those matters pertaining to spiritual existence.

My way or God's way

My way with no regard for God could be problematic and debilitating for relationships. In fact, a person who disregards a relationship with God, which renews and transforms the mind, could be very toxic in interpersonal associations. Events could be interpreted through the lens of self—what is in it for me? In fact, contents of the mind—God or self—determine the meaning of daily and yearly events in the relationship. "The belief that our feelings are caused by external events is not the whole truth. It is only a piece of the puzzle. The emotions you experience are created by the meanings you attribute to the events. You decide what each event means to you."[13]

If the mind is engaged with God—revelation of Jesus Christ, the Holy Spirit, and God's Word—then correct thinking will contribute to meanings of events that build relationships. For instance, in the many painful events of Joseph's life, he used the lens of God and his word to provide meaning for the events. In fact, God was the ground of his aspirations. He said, "You intended to harm me, but God intended it for good, to accomplish what is now being done, the saving of lives."[14] One has to understand that events can go against

---

[11] Robert E. Webber, *The Church In The World: Opposition, Tension or Transformation?* (Grand Rapids, MI: Zondervan Publishing House, 1986), 17

[12] Ibid., 108.

[13] James Creighton, *How Loving Couples Fight* (Fairfield, CN: Aslan Publishing, 1990), 43.

[14] Genesis 50: 20.

the relationship with the possibility of severing faith in God, and pushes the marriage to divorce (Romans 8: 35–39). The temptation to move away from God and your spouse and go it alone is a relentless effort of Satan to get one to do the wrong thing.

When one brings the thinking of "my way or the highway" into the relationship, the joys and happiness of the relationship soon evaporate. In most instances of interaction, one often lashes out to stay in control. The thinking is "who are you to stand in the way of what I want to do?" Adam and Eve may have thought that God was standing in the way of what they wanted—to be like God knowing good and evil. So, they rebelled against God. Lucifer thought that God was standing in the way of what he wanted so he rebelled against God.

By blaming his wife and not taking responsibility, Adam interpreted the situation in the interest of self in order to remain in control. This response is a power move. Power is used in relationships in a number of ways to win verbal fights. One of the uses of power to get one's way is blaming. However, blaming does not address the issue of conflict, and therefore, the fight continues. In an act of amazing grace, God stepped in and provided a hopeful solution to the human dilemma. God said, "I will put enmity between you and the woman, and between your offspring and hers; he will crush your head and you will strike his heel.[15] While God took the responsibility to resolve the issue of human sin and rebellion, human beings would accept responsibility for addressing the interpersonal fissures in the relationship, and do so under the authority of God. As such, God said to the woman, "I will greatly increase your pain in childbearing; with pain you will give birth to children. Your desire shall be for your husband and he will rule over you."[16]

The responsibility should be carried out in an attitude of care, comfort, and love. "A careful distinction is maintained between human-kind's dominion over the animals and the husband's 'rule' over his wife. Furthermore, although the verb *masal* does consistently indicate submission, subjection, or dominion in scripture "the idea of tyrannous exercise of power does not lie in the verb."[17] Davidson writes, "In fact there are many passages where *masal* is used with the connotation of 'rule' in the sense of 'comfort, protect, care for, and love.'"[18]

---

[15] Genesis 3:15.

[16] Genesis 3:16.

[17] Richard M. Davidson, *The Theology of Sexuality In The Beginning: Genesis 1-2* Andrews University Seminary Studies, Spring 1988, Vol. 26 No. 1. 5–24 (Michigan: Andrews University Press, 1988) 128. Davidson quoted John Skinner, *Genesis*, ICC (Edinbugh, 1930), 53.

Accepting responsibility for failure is the best way forward to a brighter future, notwithstanding the pain that may accompany that noble duty.

> We need to face that we have failed. Until we do we can find ourselves sinking deeper and deeper into darkness tied to the past rather than rising to a brighter future. Our long-term success may well depend on our accepting, in the short run, when failure is really failure.[19]

Both God and human beings suffer the agony resulting from broken relationships. Yet accepting responsibility is still the best way forward. Notwithstanding the pain of reproduction, each would desire to stay together.

Another use of power to get one's way is defensiveness. Defensiveness is often evidenced by emotional outbursts accompanied with a flood of invalidating words spewed out in order to shut down another person.[20] This lethal action could maim a person emotionally and spiritually. When one is defending herself or himself by using power to get their way, the relational wounds and emotional carnage could be overwhelming. This is an unhealthy use of power because the relationship suffers. "What causes fights and quarrels among you? Don't they come from your desires that battle within you? You want something but don't get it. You kill and covet, but you cannot have what you want. You quarrel and fight. You do not have because you do not ask God."[21] When God is not consulted or when we act like we don't have to take someone outside of ourselves into account, our relationships shatter.

A mind for relationship

The problems in relationships have more to do with the war within our own minds than communication, compatibility, love, temperament, genogram, and emotional stability.[22] To have a mind for relationship is to acknowledge sinfulness, seek forgiveness, and prostrate ourselves before the God who

---

[18] Ibid, 128 (2 Samuel 23:3; Proverbs 17:2; Isaiah 40:10; Isaiah 63:19; Zechariah 6:13. Cf Robert D. Culver).

[19] Charles Manz, *The Power of Failure* (San Francisco: Barrett-Koehler Publishers, Inc., 2002), 78.

[20] Luke 22:54–62

[21] James 4:1–2.

[22] Dave Harvey, *When Sinners Say "I Do": Discovering the Power of the Gospel for Marriage* (PA: The Shepherds Press, 2007), 31.

created us and redeemed us. God first made us in his image.[23] The intention was for relationship.

In fact, God created male and female with intellect, emotion and a will.[24] These Godlike personality qualities equipped Adam and Eve for a relationship with God and with one another. From its inception, though, rebellion against God has made relationships on the human level a struggle. Kostenberger describes the difficulty by writing,

> Marriage is shown to be rooted in God's creative act of making humanity in his image as male and female. Sin is depicted as the result of humanity's rebellion against the Creator, at the instigation of Satan, himself a fallen creature, and as becoming so much a part of human nature that people ever since the fall are by nature rebelling against their Creator and his plan for their lives.[25]

The rebellion can be abated when God and his Word are received in the mind (Matt. 4:1–11). In humble surrender, human beings open up the mind to the revelation of God. The grace he extends pardons sin and appropriate forgiveness to the sinners. As sinners, we now see our undone state and the riches of the grace of God. The Glory of God will correct the mind and fit it for relationship (2 Cor. 5:17). This experience requires a humble mind (James 4:6–10).

"There are two things that can humble the soul of men, a due consideration of God and ourselves. Of God in in his greatness, glory, holiness, power, majesty and authority; of ourselves in our mean, abject and sinful condition."[26] Instead of man having his way, God will have his way, and the purpose for which God established relationship would be realized. Marital relationships are for the glory of God. The Westminster Shorter Catechism informs us in the human struggle. "What is the chief end of man? A man's chief end is to glorify God and to enjoy him forever." Notwithstanding this truth, the stubbornness of rebellion appears to latch on to human nature in perpetuity. Yet the grace of

---

[23] Genesis 1:26–28.

[24] Andreas J. Kostenberger, *God, Marriage and Family: Rebuilding the Biblical Foundation* (Wheaton IL: Crossway, 2010), 23.

[25] Ibid., 22

[26] John Owen, *Sin and Temptation*, abridged and editedby James M. Houston (Vancouver, B.C: Regent, 1995), xvii.

God can keep self-seeking in check. "Human sin is stubborn but not stubborn as the grace of God and not half so persistent, not half so ready to win its way."[27] The tendency of having my way can be avoided when we have God in our mind, and his word becomes normative in the daily events our lives (Psalm 119:9–11).

Self-fulfillment behaviors should be eliminated by automatically engaging the mind of God (2 Peter 1:4). Mohler writes about the need for convictional intelligence in leadership in order to operate out of habits of the mind that are connected to Christian Truth and knowledge, intellectual reflexes that correspond to biblical truth and intuition that helps one to do what he knows is right in complicated situations.[28] In like manner, couples in marriage should connect habits of the mind to God and his truth. Intellectual reflexes should correspond to the Word of God, and intuition should motivate a spouse to do what is right because he or she knows it's the right thing to do, even in complicated events. The tendencyof having my way should be conquered with a preoccupation with God and his revelation (Romans 8:37).

Discussion Questions

1. Why, in interpersonal relationships, is the question about taking into account someone outside of us so important?
2. In relationships, when persons can't get their own way, they tend to rebel against those whom they identify as blocking their path. What can we learn after viewing the brokenness that results from self-interest?
3. Taking responsibility for failure tends to be the best way forward. Why do you think many persons prefer to blame and become defensive?
4. A mind needs to be ready for relationship. Explain the Gospel process that prepares the mind for relationship.
5. Considering that we all struggle with incorrect thinking and self-centeredness, how is this chapter beneficial to you?

---

[27] Cornelius Plantinga, *Not The Way It's Suppose To Be: A Breviary of Sin*, (Grand Rapids, MI: Wm. B. Eerdsman Pub. Com., 1995), 199.

[28] Albert Mohler, *The Conviction to Lead: 25 Principles for Leadership that Matters*, (Minneapolis, Minnesota: Bethany House Publishers, 2012), 33–35.

Chapter Two

Ⓦ

The tryrannous "I don't care what you think."

Moral character is assessed not by what a man knows but by what he loves. —Augustine[29].

Many times, in an almost routine way, we think one thing and do another. In fact, it is possible in our minds to replace the things of God with the things of men and proceed to act in ways contrary to the things of God. One of the acts against God is to disregard what others are thinking. This is true in the private sacred space of marriage, as well as in the broader public space of the church. For instance, in the second Great Awakening, the American political ethos invaded the minds of revivalists to the point that they inadvertently denounced responsible learning through a system of education, in their assault on the privileged class of priest and general ecclesiastical authority.[30] While not intending to overthrow education, by advancing the political view of "unalienable rights" in ecclesiastical matters, the masses felt that they were free to think how they wished without referring to persons who were tried, proven, and educated. The Revivalists promulgated the political ethos, to the detriment of biblical understanding of the teaching learning process (Ephesians 4: 8–16).

---

[29] Henry Chadwick, *Augustine: A Short Introduction* (Oxford: oxford University Press, 2001), 54.

[30] Nancy Pearcy, points out, "The priesthood of all believers was taken to mean religion of the people, by the people and for the people." Nancy Pearcy, *Total Truth: Liberating Christianity from Its Cultural Captivity* (Wheaton, IL: Crossway, 2005), 275.

Gordon Wood called this condition *"an epistemological crisis."*[31.] The individual felt he could make decisions without reference to the informed input of any educated person. Often in marriages, the input of the other spouse is disregarded in a form of liberation that goes completely against the will of God. It violates the relational and social dimension of the marriage. "When God created the woman, he declared, 'It is not good that man should be alone; I will make him a helper fit for him'" (Genesis 2:18). God proceeded to fashion a woman from one of the man's ribs and brought her to the man who exclaimed, "This at last is bone of my bones and flesh of my flesh; she shall be called Woman, because she was taken out of Man" (Genesis 2:21–23). Thus the male-female relationship, including its sexual component, serves also the purpose of alleviating man's aloneness and of providing companionship, resulting in the man and the woman becoming "one flesh" (Genesis 2:24)."[32.] Two thinking beings, brought together before God, in a sacred rite, for a lifetime of mutual commitment and reflection.

Mutual reflection or thinking together on complex marital issues is an important component of marital commitment. Spouses should bring to bear the things of God on the issue at hand. God and his Word provide a framework for integrating understanding and thinking correctly about issues of conflict. Just as the world has its problems, so also marriage has its share of relational issues. Running away or avoiding thinking together to bring biblical solutions to conflict issues is tantamount to simply hoping that the problem would go away if you run and hide. When Adam and Eve hid themselves, the problem was not solved.

To get up from a complex issue and storm out is never the answer. If two are committed to think together, in the light of God's existence, no one needs to leave in despair. On the other hand, no one needs to trivialize the issue. Hard and correct thinking are needed for serious issues of relationships. John Stott challenges Christians not to despair in the face of the mounting woes of the world by stating, "Such despair denigrates God, because it denies the usefulness of his revelation, as a lamp to our feet and a light to our path (Psalm 119:105). To abandon hope of having nothing to say may even be mental

---

[31.] Gordon S. Wood, *The Radicalism of The American Revolution: How A Revolution Transformed A Monarchical Society Into A Democratic One Unlike Any That Have Ever Existed* (New York: Knopf, 1992), 361–362.

[32.] Kostenberger, p. 81.

laziness in the guise of false humility."[33] In like manner, God has equipped married believers with resource that can be brought to bear on all problems. "His Divine power has given us everything we need for life and Godliness through our knowledge of him who called us by his own glory and goodness" (2 Peter 1:3). Therefore, both have something to say on the conflict issues and should care about what each other think.

The enemy within

Too often a spouse may be doing great damage to the marriage and at the same time resistant to hearing the other spouse's thoughts. However, if the truth is not spoken and received, the damage to the marriage could be irreparable— damage done from within. This is demonstrable on the wider landscape of human relationships as well. For instance, heterosexual intellectuals during the rise of modernity worked assiduously to dismantle structures such as marriage and family.[34] But conservative Christians seem silent on the issue.

> Conservative Christians far too quickly accuse the proponents of same-sex marriage of being the enemies of marriage, believing that marriage was in great shape before same-sex couples started clamoring for legal recognition of their unions. This is intellectual dishonesty, and the record must be set straight. The previous damage to marriage can be traced to the intellectual, sexual, legal and therapeutic subversion of marriage by *heterosexuals*.[35]

Many times, we do not see the enemy within. And because we don't see or choose not to see, we need someone else to speak truth to us.

God walked into the garden and called for Adam and began to confront him with truth in the form of questions. "Where are you? ... Who told you

---

[33] John Stott, *Decisive Issues Facing Christianity Today* (New Jersey: Fleming H. Revell company, 1990), 30.

[34] Brigitte Berger and Peter L. Berger write, "Modernity, in particular has developed a keen sense of privacy, and modern individuals are particularly prone to being shocked when private matters come to be publicly exhibited." Brigitte Berger and Peter L. Berger, *The War Over the Family: Capturing the Middle Ground* (New York: Anchor Press, 1983), 4. The family was problematized and politicized.

[35] R. Albert Mohler, Jr., *We Cannot Be Silent: Speaking Truth to a Culture Redefining Sex, Marriage & and The Very Meaning of Right and Wrong,* (Nashville, TN: Nelson Books, 2015), 89.

that were naked? ... Have you eaten from the tree that I commanded you not to eat from?" (Genesis 3:9–11) The questions were designed to get to the truth. God cannot be silent; so, in matters of truth, believers should not be silent.

"I don't care what you think" is relational tyranny that keeps one spouse in darkness and strikes fear into the other partner to be silent and remain fearful (John 3:19–21). Darkness and silence work against the integrity of the marriage and encourage an environment for hurting behaviors. The map in the mind is being changed to suit the situation. This leads to incorrect thinking that ensues into acts against the one you love. "The sequence is compelling. If we want to live straight, we have to think straight. If we want to think straight, we have to have renewed minds. For once our minds are renewed, we shall become preoccupied not with the way of the world but with the will of God, which will change us."[36] Thinking straight is synonymous with correct thinking.

Vigilance is needed to prevent self-inflicted wounds on the marriage. Couples should discover quickly that they could become the most dangerous threat to the marriage. In the War of 1812, Commodore Perry reported, "We have met the enemy and they are us." He said that to William Henry Harrison after the Battle of Lake Erie. In a cartoon created in 1970, cartoonist Walt Kelly revised the quote to, "We have met the enemy and he is us."[37] Every couple should be aware of this truth in the marriage. Like nations, empires, and governments, many times marriages fall from within when the thoughts of others are disregarded.

Acts against the one you love
Writing about the paradox of man, John Stott laments, "We can behave like God in whose image we were made only to descend to the level of the beasts. We are able to think, choose, create, love and worship, but also to refuse to think, to choose evil, to destroy, to hate, and to worship ourselves."[38] This kind of incongruence elevates the need for sharing thoughts and truth telling in the marriage. However, codependency and separation anxiety could prevent the truth from being told and thoughts from being shared. Notwithstanding,

[36] John Stott, p. 32.

[37] IRIS, Business Growth, "We have met the Enemy and He is us" May 07, 2018. Chris Ruisi challenges businesses to look inward instead of at their outward competition. In 1970 the first Earth Day was celebrated. The cartoonist Walt Kelly identified man as the enemy of the earth.

[38] John Stott, p. 38

love demands that truth be spoken to awaken spouses to moral responsibility. It is a moral responsibility for mates to care about how each other thinks on a matter. No need for a spouse to give in to codependence.

"Co-dependence is any attempt to ignore, and thereby reinforce, another's weaknesses."[39] Marriages bump into some problems that we cannot simply dance around in order to keep the marriage together. Neither is it productive to become afraid that your spouse may leave you if you speak up and say what you think.

> Separation anxiety may creep up on us whenever we shift to a more autonomous, non-blaming position in a relationship, or even when we simply consider the possibility. Such anxiety is based on a realistic fear that if we assume a bottom-line stance (I am sorry but I will not do what you are asking of me), we risk losing a relationship or a job.[40]

Feeling that your spouse doesn't care what you think could be quite worrisome. However, silence will bring monumentally more pain than telling the truth and sharing your thoughts.

There are many issues that if left unattended would bring enormous agony to the marriage. At this point I will mention addiction and infidelity. Let's look at addiction.

> By definition, the addict replaces normal human relationships with compulsive behavior that is out of control. If you are married to an addict, you feel the loss, you try to deny it exists, and you become angry. In spite of your despair—or perhaps because of it—you go to extreme lengths to preserve the exterior world of your addicted spouse and your once-happy home.[41]

---

[39] David Hawkins, *9 Critical Mistakes Most Couples Make: Identify the Pitfalls and Discover God's Help,* (Oregon: Harvest House Publishers, 2005), 58.

[40] Harriet Lerner, *The Dance of Anger,* (New York: HarperCollins, 19850, 97.

[41] Drs. Les & Leslie Parrott, *When Bad Things Happen To Good Marriages: How to Stay Together When Life Pulls You Apart,* (Grand Rapids, MI: Zondervan Publishing House, 2001), 111.

Yet, it is felt that your spouse doesn't care what you think. Confronting your spouse with truth is an easier burden to carry than the weight of denial. As a thinking being, saying something will counteract the toxicity.

Self-discipline and honesty will rule the day in the end. As laborious as these may seem, they contribute to transparency and openness needed for relationships to succeed.

> Yet the rewards of the difficult life of honesty and dedication to the truth are more than commensurate with the demands. By virtue of the fact that their maps are continually being challenged, open people are continually growing people. Through their openness they can establish and maintain intimate relationships far more effectively than closed people.[42]

It's a gain and not a loss to openly and honestly expose issues and address them seriously, even when a spouse appears as though he doesn't care how you think.

As it relates to infidelity, many spouses have felt this blow in the solar plexus of their marriage. In 1998 a research shows 24 percent of men and 14 percent of women have stepped out of their marriage in sexual affairs.[43] The hurt of adultery is not easy to overcome. Being quiet and going in hiding may not be the best way to heal the marriage. Once you are in possession of the facts that your spouse is cheating, it is wise to not to enable your adulterous spouse. Living a lie in the shadows is no life that glorifies God. Inflicting hurt in marriage is not acceptable. "The more honest one is, the easier it is to continue being honest, just as the more lies one has told, the more necessary it is to lie again. By their openness, people dedicated to truth live in the open, and through the exercise of their courage to live in the open, they become free from fear."[44] Liberation from fear comes through openness and honesty. Couples should challenge themselves to care about what each other think.

The tyranny of "I don't care what you think" should not be taken without push back. Any spouse who isolates himself places himself and the marriage in grave danger (Genesis 3:1–5). God placed Adam and Eve together in Eden

---

[42] M. Scott Peck, *The Road Less Travelled: A New Psychology of Love, Traditional Values and Spiritual Growth*, (New York: Simon & Schuster, 1978), 63.

[43] K. S. Peterson, "Affairs" *USA Today* (December 21, 1998).

[44] M. Scott Peck, 63.

to live as a team. The incomprehensible separation of the two that resulted in Eve being at the forbidden tree talking to the serpent contributed to the fall and their exit from Eden to a life fraught with pain and suffering. The motivation to protect the team is found in the words of Jesus. "Love the Lord your God with all your heart and with all your soul, and with all your mind, and with all your strength. The second is this: Love your neighbor as yourself" (Mark 12: 30–31). Each mate has a moral obligation and biblical authorization to care.

***

Discussion Questions

1. Have you ever experienced alienation in your marriage? If so, describe the experience.
2. How do the things of men replace the things of God when a conflict issue has to be dealt with in the marriage?
3. What makes "I don't care what you think" such a dangerous position in the marriage?
4. Why do you think it is difficult for married couples to see themselves as enemies of the marriage?
5. How can married folk hold one another accountable when facing human incongruity?

CHAPTER THREE

❦

The tryrannous "I listen to what pleases me."

No man is an island entire of itself: every man is part of the main.—John Donne (1572-1631)

Anyone who chooses to listen to what pleases him and turn a deaf ear to matters that challenge him is defaulting on a service owed to his spouse. In marriage, there is a lot for both spouses to listen to. Much of the issues may not be pleasant. However, the best thing to do is to listen. Listening should become a spiritual service to one another and to God. For instance, Orthland said, "If your work is difficult you may say, 'Please, when I come home I don't want to hash it all over again, I want to forget it and relax.' *But your goal is communicating, merging, feeling married, 'thinking two'!* Then pulling down the curtain on your partner means that now you've got two problems instead of one."[45] I might add, you have three problems with three persons—husband, wife, and God. Not listening contributes to problems with three persons.

As a service, listening brings wholeness to relationships. In fact, each person in the marriage should focus on the service of listening that invigorates the whole. Referencing *Life Together* by Dietrich Bonhoeffer, Bryan Craig writes, "He says that the first service we owe to others consists of listening to

---

[45] Anne Ortlund, *Building A Great Marriage* (Old Tappan, NJ: Fleming H. Revell Company, 1985), 68

19

them—that loving another person means learning to listen to them."[46] In marriage, listening is the first service owed to each other. Listening integrates relationships. Jesus said, "So, they are no longer two, but one. Therefore what God has joined together, let not men separate" (Matthew 19:6). The fact that God united a man and a woman in marriage demonstrates the utmost need for listening to one another and to God.

There is an admonition that Bonhoeffer gave to Christians in general that is applicable to married couples. He said, "But he who can no longer listen to his brother will soon be no longer listening to God either; we will be doing nothing but prattle in the presence of God too. This is the beginning of the death of the Spiritual life."[47] The service of listening to a spouse is also a service to God. How one listens to his or her spouse is an indication of the spiritual life with God. Therefore, "First seek to understand, then be understood."[48] To do this requires listening.

Obstacles in the way of listening

The Christian couple should have the habits of mind that correspond to the Word of God. James write, "My dear brothers, take note of this: Everyone should be quick to listen, slow to speak and slow to become angry" (James 1:19). Considering that communication goes beyond words to meaning, listening well prevents defensiveness that often hinders exploration of feeling, thoughts, perspectives, and ideas to get to meaning. "Unfortunately, a few people are good listeners. Even at the purely informational level, researchers claim that 75% of oral communication is ignored,misunderstood or quickly forgotten. Rarer still is the ability to listen for the deepest meanings in what people say."[49]

There should be a determined effort on the part of spouses to really want to know the other persons perspective on a life situation. "One of the primary

---

[46] Bryan Craig, *Searching For Intimacy In Marriage* (United States. General Conference, 2001), 82

[47] Dietrich Bonhoeffer, *Life Together* (London: SCM Press, Ltd., 1954), 75

[48] Stephen R. Covey, *The 7 Habits of Highly Effective People* (New York: Simon and Schuster, Inc., 1989), 236.

[49] Robert Boltman advocates, "It is helpful to know the distinction between hearing and listening. Hearing says Professor John Drakeford, "is a word used to describe the physiological sensory processes by which the auditory sensations are received by the ears and transmitted to the brain. Listening, on the other hand, refers to more complex psychological procedure, involving interpreting and understanding the significance of sensory procedures." Robert Boltman, *People Skills: How To Assert Yourself, Listen To Others, And Resolve Conflicts* (New York: Simon & Schuster, 1979), 30 see John Drakeford, *The Awsome Power of The listening Ear* (Waco, Texas: Word, 1967), 17.

tasks of a listener is to stay out of the other's way so the listener can discover how the speaker views the situation."[50] When persons get in the way, one could become defensive and ruin any desire for exploration. So, listen first then respond.

David W. Johnson exposes five responses that if rightly used could be effective against defensiveness.[51] First response is giving advice. If the timing is right, then giving advice could be effective. However, in many instances, giving advice is not rightly timed. As such, giving advice makes the spouse feel threatened and will resort to becoming closed-minded and defensive. In fact, the spouse may feel a sense of inferiority and close the door to any further advise or evaluation in order to avoid any further conflict. If a husband is communicating an issue and his wife gives untimely advice, he may feel that his spouse does not value involvement as a precious use of time. On the flip side, giving advice could hinder persons from taking responsibility for their own behaviors. When giving advice, couples need to be certain that the time is right.

The second response is analyzing or interpreting a problem. If a husband chooses to interpret the problem that his wife is communicating, he goes about as a teacher whose intention is to tell his wife what is the meaning of the problem, what is the cause of her thinking that way, and why she is behaving the way she does. Such an approach makes the wife defensive. As such, she will not share thoughts and feelings out of an abundance of fear that they will be analyzed and interpreted. It would be better to allow her to think about her thoughts and feelings in order to arrive at causes than to appear as though you know her more than she knows herself. Analyze and interpret if you are welcomed to do so.

The third response is for the spouse to be reassuring and supporting. A husband may be communicating an issue with intensity. In an effort to reduce the intensity, a wife may become reassuring and supporting. This leads to defensiveness, as the husband may feel that his feeling is just brushed aside. Here again, timing is important. There are times when the husband needs reassurance. At times it's more effective to validate the intense feeling. For example, "It appears as though you are incensed about what happened at work."

---

[50] Boltman, 40.

[51] David W. Johnson, *Reaching Out: Interpersonal Effectiveness and Self-Actualization 8th edition* (Boston, MA: Allyn and Bacon, 2003), 224. Johnson lists five ways to listen and respond. Advising and Evaluating, Analyzing and Interpreting, Reassuring and Supporting, Question and Probing, Paraphrasing and Understanding.

Don't say, "After the cross comes the crown, so calm down." "Reassurance is a way of seeming to comfort another person while doing the opposite."[52]

The fourth response is asking questions. When there is a conflict issue and the wife asks questions, it indicates that she wants to understand the issue. However, she may have a conclusion in her mind and may probe in order to get her husband to reach that conclusion. That is playing God. God asked Adam and Eve questions to get to conclusions that he already reached. When faulty human beings follow this route, they may end up asking "why" questions. Such questions could appear as advice or judgments in the mind of a spouse. In the case of this husband and wife, the husband could become defensive if he feels judged. The wife could be helped by asking questions that address "what," "how," and "when." These questions allow for exploration of thoughts and feelings. Also, the questions should be opened. For instance, "How was work today?" instead of "Do you like your job?" The wife could make reflective statements in addition to asking questions. For instance, the wife may say, "You really like what you do" instead of "Do you like your work?"

The fifth response is paraphrasing. Paraphrasing is done to understand thoughts, feelings, and meanings behind the words spoken. If a husband doesn't understand his wife's thoughts and feelings on an issue, then it's best he paraphrases. For example, "You feel annoyed that I did not return your call." This could be in response to a husband saying, "I called, and you didn't take up the phone. I don't treat you that way." In this way, the husband can hear what he just said and realize that his wife is trying to understand his thoughts and feelings. This approach prevents defensiveness. "When feelings and facts are joined in one succinct response, we have reflection of meaning."[53] The husband and wife should reach the same understanding of meaning behind the words.

Responses could become obstacles to effective listening if used without regard to timing and wisdom. Spouses can ask God for wisdom (James 1: 5). Providing insight to wives, Martha Peace writes, "Not answering back like a fool is easy to understand but hard to do in the heat of conflict. If confused, a wife does not have to immediately give her husband a direct answer since Proverbs 15:28 says, 'The heart of the righteous ponders how to answer....'" Likewise, a wife who is faced with harsh, unreasonable demands may ask him

---

[52] Robert Boltman, *People Skills*, 25.

[53] Robert Boltman, p. 57

for time to consider her answer. She might say, "I need to think about how to answer you, and I will give you a response as soon as possible." If her husband has not considered all the facts or has not gathered the information necessary to make wise decision, he may be making a rash judgment. A godly wife may respond to her husband's rash judgments concerning her by saying, "Would you please wait until I can give you more information before you…'answer a matter…' (Proverbs 18:13)."[54] Taking time to think about a matter allows for a response that is timely and wise. The service of listening could be laborious, but the relational rewards are huge.

Don't lose sight of the whole

Husbands and wives listen differently. While the woman may provide more verbal feedback, the man may be delayed in responses. Both could be misleading. On the one hand, the man feels that the woman agrees with him because when the man is in agreement, he tends to use more listening signals as the woman. This causes misunderstanding. On the other hand, the woman feels that the man is uncaring because he doesn't give as many listening responses as she would do. To avoid this mix up, a husband and wife should listen because of their care, love, and desire to be close and as an act of grace.[55]

These patterns in listening are vital for proper relational function. Marriage ought to be looked upon as a system with parts that interrelate in the interest of the whole. Systems thinking could be productive in seeing how marriage function as a whole. "Systems thinking looks at the whole, and the parts, and the connections between the parts, studying the whole in order to understand the parts."[56] Listening is part of the system of marriage. This part has patterns. Listening patterns, when understood, in relation to the whole contribute to a cohesive whole (1 Corinthians 12:14–26).

Listening is a servant of the whole. When couples value the existence of their marriage, they will take pride in listening to each other and to God. H.

---

[54] Martha Peace, *The Excellent Wife: A Biblical Perspective* (Bemidji, Minnesota: Focus Publishing Inc., 2005), 167.

[55] H. Norman Wright, *Communication: Key To Your Marriage* (Ventura, CA: Regal Books, 2000), 105–107. There are gender differences in listening styles. A woman may view a man as uninterested and interruptive; but that may not be the case. It is in the listening style of man to be delayed in responses yet challenge statements. It's best to understand the differences and use them to the advantage of both.

[56] Joseph O'Connor & Ian McDermott, *The Art Of Systems Thinking: Essential Skills for Creativity and Problem Solving* (San Francisco CA: Thorsons, 1997), 1.

Norman Wright exclaimed, "One of the greatest gifts one person can give to another is the gift of listening. It can be an act of love and caring. But far too many couple only hears one another. Few actually listen."[57] Could it be that that the deficiency of value in the whole results in the nonchalant and self-centered approach to listening? Think on these things correctly.

Couples should place a high premium on listening. Stuart Scott posits,

> A marriage is only as good as a couple's ability to send and receive the right message. But beyond its effect on the marriage, good communication is important to God. Look carefully at how you communicate, because your communication will reveal the kind of man you are. Poor, sinful communication habits must be replaced with those that please God.[58]

He went on to provide six prerequisites for good communication. One of them reads, "I must know how to listen."[59] Notice that both the spiritual life and marriage could be adversely affected by listening that is self-centered. Therefore, in listening, let us serve one another and God. This is correct thinking.

⚘

Discussion Questions

1. Can self-centered listening teach us important lessons about the Christian marriage? Can you think of biblical examples?
2. Why is listening so important for marriage and spirituality?'
3. What did you find most intriguing and provocative in this chapter?
4. Identify the six listening responses and define each one. How do you feel about them?
5. Define listening, and describe listening as a service. How does God fit in the service of listening?

---

[57] H. Norman Wright, 95

[58] Stuart Scott, *The Exemplary Husband: A Biblical Perspective* (Focus Publishing INC, 2000), 55

[59] Ibid., 56 The six prerequisites of good communication posited by Scott: 1. I must want to please God more than anything else. 2. I must be humble. 3. I must realize I am accountable to God for everything I say. 4. I must know how to listen. 5. I must know that communication involves more than just words. 6. I must be willing to spend time and effort to communicate.

6. What are some of the gender differences in listening between a man and a woman?

7. What do you think are some of the effects of listening for the purpose of satisfying the whole, than just one person?

Chapter Four

The tryrannous "I am not the problem."

What is the difference between an obstacle and an opportunity? Our attitude toward it. Every opportunity has a difficulty and every difficulty has an opportunity. —J. Sidlow Baxter

When a spouse feels personally attacked by an assertion, he may withdraw in an effort to defend himself and self-justify. In other words, the husband may become defensive. Robert Boltman describes this experience between persons as *push-push back phenomenon.*[60] Notwithstanding the reality of such phenomenon, both partners should think of the relationship as more important than personal feelings. The principle at work should be teamwork. "You have a choice when dealing with any problem. Either you will nurture a sense that you are a team working together against the problem or you will operate as though you are working against each other. This principle holds with all problems, great or small."[61]

---

[60] Robert Boltman, *People skills: How To Assert Yourself, Listen To Others and Resolve Conflicts,* 160-163 "We have a special phrase that we use to describe an assertion and the predictable defensive response to it. We call it "the push- push back phenomenon". Virtually every assertion message is experienced as a "push." Even when the assertion is only attempting to remove the other person from the asserter's territory, the confrontation is experienced as a "push." In response to that push there is almost an inevitable push back."

[61] Howard J. Markman, Scott M. Stanley, Susan L. Blumberg, *Fighting For Your Marriage* (San Francisco, California: Jossey-Bass, 2001), 156.

Relationships require strength. Thankfully, each partner could draw strength from God (Isaiah 40: 28–31). God is integrally a part of the team. So partners should gather themselves and think of the relationship as more important than defensive self- justifying feelings. While partners draw strength from God to address a disturbing issue, it is beneficial to understand the gender uniqueness and sameness that is at work.

Many men withdraw when they perceive that the issues of their wives appear unfixable. It appears as though women tend to bring up issues more frequently than men. While men withdraw because they believe the problem is unfixable, women, for the most part, raise issues simply for men to give a listening ear, not to fix their problem.[62] It is vitally important for partners to think through responses before reacting. For instance, if a wife asserts, "When we plan to take summer vacation and you put it off, I feel upset because I think that I am not valued more than your work." Instead of pushing back, it's more productive to listen and seek an appointment to completely address the issue. In this way, there is no withdrawal.

Teaming up to address problems

The enemy of marriage is self. Problems should not be conflated with personal acceptance or rejection. Instead of creating distance and allowing the problem to prevail, the couple should unite as team to break up the problem in manageable pieces and give sufficient time to address the problem piece by piece. This approach requires a spiritual attitude. "The natural heart wants to have its way. We do not like to be told what to do. We are naturally rebellious and selfish. The conflict then results in angry outburst, pouting, manipulating, nagging, or resentment."[63]

Therefore, both should be diligent in the preservation of the oneness, in the unity of the Spirit in the bond of peace (Ephesians 4:1–3). Martha Peace sees in Ephesians 4:1–3 attitudes needed to solve conflict in marriage. These are Humility, Gentleness, Patience, and Forbearance. When one is humble, he recognizes that he is accountable to one above him. In this sense, a partner ceases to seek his own way and look for ways to glorify God in the marriage. Gentleness is evidenced in compassion and thoughtfulness in responses. In

---

[62] Ibid., It is more productive for a one spouse to listen to what is upsetting her partner and resist the urge to solve problems.

[63] Martha Peace, *The Excellent Wife*, p. 199.

fact, gentleness replaces manipulation, harsh tone, and sarcasm. Patience prevails in tests and trials. Marriage could be a sanctifying experience, and thus, patience provides the capacity to listen and respond in productive ways. Forbearance helps both spouses to put up with one another. God helps the couple to put up with one another in conflicts.

Too many times couples seem so geared up to separate when differences arise. Husbands and wives are to become one not uniformed. God created male and female. As such there is diversity. Both identities should remain differentiated and not enmeshed. Being different presupposes that each person sees things differently. Sadly, human nature, because of sin, resists diversity. "The natural instinct is to create distance between us and the ones who are different."[64] Therefore, couples need to request strength from God every day to preserve the oneness of marriage in the unity of the Spirit.

In fact, when couples accept that they think differently, feel differently, and have different likes and dislikes, they are in a stronger position to work through conflict issues. Such acceptance demonstrates a trait of genuine love.

> The genuine lover always perceives the beloved as someone who has a totally separate identity. Moreover, the genuine lover always respects and even encourages this separateness, and the unique individuality of the beloved. Failure to perceive and respect this separateness is extremely common, however, and the cause of much mental illness and unnecessary suffering.[65]

Such a posture of accepting separateness in identity is disarming and allows couples to self-disclose in more forthcoming ways because the environment is safe.

Markman Stanley and Blumberg offer some practical steps for handling problems well. They suggest problem discussion and problem solution.[66] "Full discussion clarifies the issues, removes conflicts, and increases feeling of teamwork. Solutions flow naturally from working together against problems rather than working against one another."[67] Discussion should take place in

---

64. Dennis B. Guernsey, *The Family Covenant: Love and Forgiveness In The Christian Home* (Pasadena, California: Hope Publishing House, 1984), 10.

65. M. Scott Peck, *The Road Less Travelled* (New York: Simon and Schuster, 1978), 160-161.

66. Markman, Stanley, Blumberg, *Fighting For Your Marriage* p. 163–170.

67. Ibid., 163.

an environment of mutual acceptance and respect. Before trying to solve problems, allow sufficient time for discussion. Both partners should talk safely and listen clearly. When the issue is being discussed, all emotional noise should be disclosed clearly. After discussion, both should now be on the same team to tackle problems. In preparation for problem solution, there should be mutual agenda outlining the specific problem to be resolved. There should be brainstorming, agreement and compromise, and follow-up.

As it relates to brainstorming, resist the temptation to criticize anyone's ideas. Simply put the ideas out and have one spouse take notes. Any idea is allowed. When it comes to agreement and compromise, expect some differences to emerge. "You are not ever going to have a great marriage if you insist on getting your way all the time. The two of you nurture a great marriage when you can put the needs of the relationship above your individual desires at key times of life."[68] If the couple reaches a solution, then the problem ends. However, if no solution is arrived at, then there is a need to follow up as a means of accountability. Follow-up should be planned and executed. Whoever fails to plan, plans to fail.

Can two walk together if they don't agree?

According to Amos 3:3, "Do two walk together unless they have agreed to do so?" Bacchiocchi points out, "When a couple marries, two cultures come together. Each brings to marriage its different upbringing, values, habits, temperament, and expectations. The way these differences are handled determines to a large extent the success of the marriage."[69] Differences presuppose that problems in words or action will arise. The process of problem discussion and problem solution lead to mutual agreement. Agreement and compromise are needed in marriage. It takes a team, which includes God, husband, and wife, to build a strong marriage that overcomes differences (Ecclesiastes 4:9–12).Exclusive responses like "I am not the problem here" do not contribute to team building nor problem-solving.

Further, when God is left out of the team, someone in the marriage is prone to play god. This is a depressing problem. However, the one playing god does not think that he or she is the problem. The one playing god will tell the other spouse how to live his life. It is self-centered approach. Harriet

---

[68] Ibid., 169.

[69] Samuel Bacchiocchi, *The Marriage Covenant: A Biblical Study on Marriage, Divorce and Remarriage* (Berrien Springs, Michigan: Biblical Perspectives, 1992), 93.

Goldhor Lerner, in her book *The Dance Of Intimacy*, called such spouses with this problem overfunctioners.[70] Hence, instead of working as a team, a spouse takes the role of God to tell the other how to live his or her life, as though the spouse is incapable of doing so. The sad irony is that it's all about pleasing the one who makes himself or herself a little god. Two cannot walk together unless they agree to do so.

Lerner lists some characteristics that are common to persons who are overfunctioners.[71]

1. They know what's best for themselves and others.
2. They move in quickly to advise, fix, rescue, and take over when stress arises.
3. They have difficulty staying out of other people's issues and allowing them to struggle with their own problems.
4. They avoid worrying about their own goals and problems by focusing on the goals and problems of other people.
5. They have difficulty sharing their own vulnerable, under-functioning side, especially with those people they believe have problems.
6. They may appear to be "always reliable" or "always together."

Playing god in a marriage is a recipe for failure. No one person has all what it takes to hold a marriage together. God, husband, and wife form a team that sustains marriage through differences. Under the authority of God, couples learn how to bear one another's burdens. "We must be able to avoid the distance of pity as well as the exclusiveness of sympathy. Compassion is born when we discover in the center of our own existence not only that God is God and man is man, but also that our neighbor is our fellowman."[72] In like manner, the distance of defensiveness and self-justification and the exclusiveness of playing god only compound the tyrannical rule of "I am not the problem here." Always think team.

---

[70] Harriet Goldhor Lerner advocates, "If we overfunction, we may truly believe that God is on our side. Surely, we have done everything possible to be helpful and our greatest source of distress is the other person—who is unable or unwilling to shape up." Harriet Goldhor Lerner, *The Dance Of Intimacy* (New York: Harper and Row Publishers, 1989), 102.

[71] David Hawkins, *9 Critical Mistakes most Couples Make: Identify the pitfalls and Discover God's Help*, 98. Lerner's list of common traits is recorded in Hawkins's book.

[72] Henri Nouwen, *The Wounded Healer* (Doubleday, 1979), 41.

❦

Discussion Questions

1. Do you have appointments to address problems? What does that say about how you view problems?
2. What makes teamwork so important? What is the difference between teamwork and playing god.
3. Why spouses become overfunctioners? Describe the common traits that overfunctioners possess.
4. How do teamwork contribute to problem discussion and problem solution?
5. How do you view compromise and agreement? How can you begin to practice solving problems well?

Chapter Five

❧❧

The tryrannous "I can't afford to get hurt again."

*There have been times when I think we do not desire heaven; but
more often I find myself wondering whether, in our heart of hearts,
we have ever desired anything else.*—C.S. Lewis

In marriage, memory is at work. Too often it appears as though memory focuses more on the bad past than good experiences of the past. If there is merit in the words of Soren Kierkegaard, "Life must be lived forwards, but it can be understood only backwards," then married couples need to be aware of the tendency for the memory to recount almost automatically past hurt.

> Even though it is behind us, it is always in our rear-view mirror. And though it seems that the images of our past should grow smaller, the irony is that the farther down life's highway we travel, the closer they sometimes appear. Always just a glance away. And always glancing back at us. The images in that mirror may send us safely on our way, or they may send us crashing in a ditch. Such is the power of memories.[73]

---

[73] Ken Gire, *Windows of The Soul* (Grand Rapids, Michigan: Zondervan Publishing House, 1996), 132

If a hurting experience remains in the mirror, it could send the marriage crashing into a ditch.

Resisting the power of memory is not the answer to addressing hurt. As a couple follows the gravitational pull, go with a mind to forgive a hurt that they deemed done to them by each other, and healing will occur. Unfinished business continues to haunt and play with the minds until matters of concern are addressed. Years only make hurt looms larger. Going forward requires that the past hurt be healed (2 Kings 6:1–6). Forgiveness is potent medicine for hurting souls.

In a world that perpetuates the law of retribution and justice, forgiveness may not be easy. The human tendency is that those who hurt us should earn forgiveness. This act of earning forgiveness is fairness for us human beings. Another challenge is that forgiveness is often turned into quid pro quo. "We make forgiveness a law of reciprocity. And this never works. For then both of us say to ourselves, 'The other fellow has to make the first move.'"[74]

In many marriages, retribution and fairness go the way of the silent treatment. This is another challenge for forgiveness. One spouse disengages because of a hurt. The fact is that the estrangement does not heal the hurt nor produce marital satisfaction. It only breeds resentment. "The word resentment expresses what happens if the cycle goes uninterrupted. It means, literally 'to feel again': resentment clings to the past, relives it over and over, pick each fresh scab so that the wound never heals."[75]

The silent treatment could sink into a bitterness that adversely affects intimacy.

> Bitterness is one of the most common causes of neglected sex. From the soil of anger and unresolved conflicts, it grows quickly into a virulent weed that chokes out intimacy. Married people turned bitter use their bodies as weapon, a weapon that harms by withholding. A weapon used to punish the other person for sinning against us. This calls for forgiveness.[76]

---

[74] Philip Yancey, *What's So Amazing About Grace?* (Grand Rapids, MI: Zondervan Publishing House, 1997), 91. Quote found in Helmut Thielicke, *Waiting*, op. cit., p.112.

[75] Ibid., 97.

[76] Dave Harvey, *When Sinners Say I Do: Discovering The Power of The Gospel for Marriage* (Wapwallopen, PA: Shepherd Press, 2007), 165.

Notwithstanding the challenges one may face to actually forgive, it is best for oneself and the marriage to take the initiative to forgive.

An approach to the future

Couples should choose the future over the past. God has done that for us. God removed the sin of the past and gives us his righteousness (Romans 5:1–5). Sin remains in the past, and righteousness equips believers for the future (Micah 7:19). God gave up his right and paid the price for sin, forgives us, and makes a new heaven and a new earth available to us (Philippians 2:5–11; Isaiah 65:17). God restores us to himself as sons and daughters and begins to recreate in us his image (2 Corinthians 5:17; Romans 8:14–18).

> Judgment and punishment face toward the past. Mercy and forgiveness face toward the future. It is a future with a cross etched into it as a reminder that we are to live with one another in mercy and forgiveness. We are to bear in mind God's merciful and forgiving act toward us in Christ. Because of the cross we can face the future and not to be captured by the past, neither the past with our own sins, nor the past with disappointments and hurts inflicted by others.[77]

An offended spouse should always be mindful that God gave her a future notwithstanding her failure. Therefore, giving her spouse a future by forgiving him actually gives the marriage and herself a future. Forgiveness sets people free, and first to be set free is the one who forgives. However, forgiveness is not just resolving negative feelings in the person who experienced hurt and actually forgives. Forgiveness is a meaningful commitment between two persons.[78] Couples should make a commitment that they would "think three"

---

[77] Denis B. Guernsey, *The Family covenant: Love and Forgiveness in the Christian Home* (Pasadena, CA: Hope Publishing House, 1984), 17.

[78] Chris Brauns *Unpacking Forgiveness: biblical answers for complex questions and deep wounds* (Wheaton, IL: Crossway, 2008), 65. There is a distinction between Biblical Forgiveness and Therapeutic Forgiveness. Braun assigned the term Therapeutic Forgiveness to Lewis Smedes redefinition of forgiveness. For Smedes, forgiveness is to cease resentment or anger over an offence. See Lewis Smedes *Forgive and Forget: Healing the Hurts We Don't Deserve*, 1984. Forgiveness deals with not just feelings but truth, commitment, and reconciliation. Offence needs to be identified and worked through. It's not enough just to resolve feelings of resentment.

in every aspect of their relationship. Anne Ortlund provides couples with correct practical approach she calls "think two." She contends,

> The philosophy behind "thinking one" is "I am on the throne; I am out first. Above all I want independence. I must be free to be my own person, to pursue what I want, to develop my self, to take care of my own needs first—I must even be free to cut myself loose from anyone, spouse or otherwise, who hinders me.[79]

Too often forgiveness is along the line of "thinking one." Thinking one never works in marriage.

While I applaud "think two," I see greater benefit in "think three" in this matter of forgiveness. Husbands and wives need to remember that God graciously forgave them, and so, in their responsibility to forgive one another, they should bring God to the experience and give one another what God has given to each of them.

God is absolutely needed because forgiveness involves forbearing one another in love (Ephesians 4: 1–30). When an offense is committed against a spouse, immediately there is a stumbling block. The couple has to cooperate with God to get passed the offence. In this process, the couple does not simply disregard the offence but makes a decision to clear the sin in the interest moving the relationship forward.

> "Forbearance applies to specific instances of sin. It involves a clear-eyed realization that we may have been sinned against, and then a bold-hearted, gospel-inspired decision to cover that sin with love. Peter gives us the key to forbearance. "Above all, keep loving one another earnestly, since love covers a multitude of sins" (1 Peter 4:8)."[80]

As the offense is defined, it is helpful to figure out if the offense is personal or substantive. Personal offenses have to do with how people feel they are treated during interpersonal interaction. Substantive offenses are major responsibilities

---

[79] Anne Ortlund, *Building A Great Marriage* (Old Tappan, Fleming H. Revell Company, 1985), 52.

[80] Dave Harvey, 88-89.

of commitment in the marriage. For instance, marital infidelity is a substantive issue. If the offense is minor, then it should be overlooked for the glory of God and the interest of the relationship. When an offense causes tension and separation between husband and wife and, at the same time, ruptures the relationship with God, such an offense should not be overlooked.

There are some offenses, though, that are better overlooked.

> Overlooking is not a passive process in which you simply remain silent for the moment but file away the offense for later use against someone. That is actually a form of denial that can easily lead to brooding over the offense and building up internal bitterness and resentment that will eventually explode in anger. Instead, overlooking is an active process that is inspired by God's mercy through the Gospel. To truly overlook an offense means to deliberately decide not to talk about it, dwell on it, or let it grow into pent-up bitterness.[81]

There may be some offenses that may be too serious to overlook. In such cases, couples should agree to invite someone who is able to equip them to work through the hurt (Ephesians 4:8–11; Matthew 18: 15–17).

It is vitally important not to forget God's role in the process. As an act of faith, the offended leaves the matter in God's hand for him to bring about justice. In his own time, God will bring about justice. "Do not take revenge, my friends; but leave room for God's wrath, for it is written: 'it is mine to avenge, I will repay'" (Romans 12:19). Forgiveness is not earned, but offered as a gift. The process may not be automatic, as the offender would have to receive the gift. Always keep in mind that vengeance belongs to God.

> Christians should offer grace to all people. We should wrap up forgiveness as a present and make it available to anyone who will accept, regardless of the offense. But it is not the offense that conditions forgiveness but the repentant heart.

---

[81] Ken Sande, *The Peace Maker: A Biblical Guide to Resolving Personal conflict* (Grand Rapids: MI: Baker Books, 2004), 83.

Whether or not they unwrap the present and accept the gift
so that forgiveness takes place is up to them.[82]

Forgiveness offered and received saves the marriage and frees the offended
and offender to glorify God in the marriage.

Concerns about rights

When the hurt becomes the measure of all things, concerns about rights loom
large. "By forgiving another, I am trusting that God is the better justice-maker
than I am. By forgiving, I release my own right to get even and leave all issues
of fairness for God to work out. I leave in God's hands the scales that must
balance justice and mercy."[83] There are times when in a marriage rights should
be talked about and respected. The concerns of rights should be seen in the
context of glorifying God and sustaining the marriage. When the issue of
rights is raised for self-advancement, the relationship becomes strained. So,
do to others what you would have them do to you (Matthew 5:12).

Ken Sande sees rights in the context of stewardship. He says,

> Rights are not something you deserve or possess for your
> own benefit. Rather they are privileges given to you by God,
> and he wants you to use them for his glory and the benefit of
> others, especially by helping them to know Christ. As a
> steward it is also appropriate to consider your needs and
> personal responsibilities (Philippians 2:3–4).[84]

There are a few metrics offended spouses could use to determine whether to
exercise rights or give up their rights. Ken Sande puts them this way:

1. Will exercising my rights honor God by showing the power of the
   Gospel in my life?
2. Will exercising my rights advance God's kingdom—or will it advance
   only my interests at the expense of his kingdom?
3. Will exercising my rights benefit others?

---

[82] Chris Brauns, 147

[83] Philip Yancey p. 93.

[84] Ken Sande, 94. The questions should be asked when one faces the concerns about rights.

4.   Is exercising my rights essential to my own well-being?

Concerns about motives

"Thinking three" is a useful organizing theme for marriage. Relationship, and not rights, seems to be the most productive motive to forgive. Motive has an effect on the forward movement of any relationship that requires forgiveness as a means of restoration. The fact that trust has been broken and grief keeps the experience alive in the mind, motivation to save the relationship is more effective than freeing oneself by exercising rights.

It is readily evident that in a situation of marital infidelity, the event will not be forgotten, even though forgiveness is extended to the offender. The fact that trust has been broken and the offended has lost something of significant worth means the experience will become part of the memory. This experience is all a part of grief. Thus, motive for forgiveness is vital at moments when past hurt seek to derail the forward march of the marriage.

If the relationship is the motive behind forgiveness, then the offended opens the door for restoration of the marriage. At the same time, if relationship were the motive for the offender who received the forgiveness, then the offender would take responsibility for the wrong committed against the other partner.

Markman, Stanley, and Blumberg point out the connection between motive for forgiveness and restoration of marriage. They explain,

> One of the most obvious reasons to forgive others is that it frees you up to move into the future. However, researchers like McCollough and Everett Worthington Jr. at Virginia Commonwealth University have been studying forgiveness, and they are finding that when people forgive mostly for personal benefit, forgiveness doesn't seem to hold up so well over time. The kind of forgiveness that lasts is that which is motivated by your desire to enhance the well-being of your mate—in these researchers' words, by the desire to be a "blessing" to the other. This is the powerful kind of sacrifice that helps restore relationships.[85]

---

[85] Howard J. Markman, Scott M. Stanley, Susan L. Blumberg, *Fighting For Your Marriage*, 315.

In marriage, forgiveness should be about the restoration of relationship where both spouses come on a level field to begin their new start toward the future. If the motive is simply freeing oneself, then God may not be glorified in the marriage. No one condones hurt in relationships. However, it is impossible not to get hurt, minor or major, in as close a relationship as marriage. In fact, the persons closest to you could hurt you the most (Genesis 3:1–15). Thus, dosages of forgiveness motivated by reconciliation could be the restorer of the breach and the end of estrangement.

Biblical Steps to forgiveness and reconciliation
1. Examine yourself (Psalm 51:3–4; 1 John 3:4; James 2:10–11; Matthew 12:1–5).
2. Remember the Golden Rule (Matthew 7:12).
3. Plan a couples meeting to discuss the sin that needs forgiveness (Matthew 18:15–17).
4. Both should explore the violation and confess sins (1 John 1:9).
5. There should be an unequivocal call for repentance (Luke 22:54–62).
6. The offender should ask for forgiveness and admit to specific wrongdoing and say, "I am sorry for hurting you by committing this wrong" (Luke 15: 17–24).
7. The offender should acknowledge wrongdoing without any excuses. Take responsibility and accept consequences (Luke 15:19; Luke 19:8).
8. The offended should offer forgiveness. The wrongdoing will be relegated to the past and will not come up in future arguments (Matthew 6:14–15).
9. The offender should be willing to make amends and change in patterns of behavior (Luke 19:8).
10. Make a commitment to be accountable to one another and to God for spiritual and physical well-being (Philippians 1:6; 2 Peter 1:4; Psalm 139:23–24; Ephesians 4:22–32; Psalm 37:4; Ezekiel 36:25–26; 2 Timothy 3: 14–17.
11. Be patient but put what is learned into practice (2 Peter 1:4–8).

Discussion Questions

1. What role does memory plays in hurt? What kind of impact does memory have on marital relationship?
2. What are the challenges posed to forgiveness? What is the meaning of resentment?
3. How should couples look at rights in a marriage? Describe the metrics that should inform the declaration of rights?
4. What did you learn from the approach of "think three"? Explain the role of God in this organizing theme.
5. Why is it important to have the right motive for forgiveness?
6. What biblical steps of forgiveness are meaningful to you? Why?

Chapter Six

❧❧

The tryrannous "I am right and you are wrong."

Those who are weell have no neeed of a physician, but those who are sick. I have not come to call the righteous but sinners to repentance.—Luke 5:31-32

In many marriages, the modus operandi seems to be that of one spouse belittling the other for the purpose of self-exaltation. The thought of self-righteousness has much to do with this mode of behavior. The parable that Jesus spoke about the Pharisee and the tax collector, Luke 18:9–14, bears out how self-righteousness manifests itself in relationships—I am right, and you are wrong.

To some who were confident of their own righteousness and looked down on everybody else, Jesus spoke this parable. Two men went up into the temple to pray, one a Pharisee and the other a tax collector. The Pharisee stood up and prayed about himself: "God I thank you that I am not like other men— robbers, evil doers, adulterers—or even like this tax collector. I fast twice a week and give a tenth of all I get." But the tax collector stood at a distance. He would not even look up to the heavens, but beat his chest and said, "God have mercy on me a sinner." I tell you the truth this man rather than the other, went home justified before God. For everyone who exalts himself will be humbled and he who humbles himself will be exalted.

In marriage, it is of significance that each partner's life is set beside God and not beside one another. If that does not happen, almost gratuitously, a spouse can be overtaken by pride, which breeds self-righteousness; and cooperation soon gives way to competition, criticism, and judgment. "No doubt all that the Pharisee said was true. He did fast: he did meticulously give tithes; he was not as other men are; still less was he like that tax collector. But the question is not 'am I as good as my fellow-men?' The question is, 'am I as good as God.'[86] Spouses should set their lives beside the life of God instead of setting their lives beside one another. This is important to avoid overflow of one another's weaknesses into each other's lives.

Paul Tripp captures this reality well when he writes about ministry in personal relationships.

> In personal ministry, the sin of the person you are helping will eventually be revealed in your relationship. If you are ministering to an angry person, at some point that anger will be directed to you. If you are helping a person who struggles with trust, at some point she will distrust you. A manipulative person will seek to manipulate you. A depressed person will tell you he tried everything you've suggested and it didn't work. You can't stand next to a puddle without eventually being splashed by its mud.[87]

This life experience takes place in marriage as well. It is a fact that human beings are all flawed (Romans 3:23). Therefore, spouses are prone to be angry, manipulative, distrustful, and draining. Further, self-righteousness is one of those weaknesses that could spill over from one spouse to another in the form of competition, criticism, and judgment. God has provided a solution to

---

[86] William Barclay, *The Gospel of Luke* The Daily Study Bible Series (Philadelphia, PA: The Westminster Press, 1975), 225.

[87] Paul Tripp, *Instruments In The Redeemer's Hands* (Phillipsburg, NJ: Presbyterian and Reformed, 2002), 136–137.

mitigate disparagement and devaluing of spouses, as well as course correct a self-righteous person. It is found in the reality that Jesus is Mediator.

> Since the coming of Christ, his followers have no more immediate realities of their own, not in their family relationships… nor in relationships formed in the process of living. Between father and son, husband and wife… stand Christ the Mediator, whether they are able to recognize him or not. We cannot establish direct contact outside ourselves except through him, through his word, and through our following him.[88]

Karen and Ron Flowers, commenting on Bonhoeffer's words, said,

> A wonderful new spiritual reality exists; Jesus Himself connects us. We are like spokes on a wheel with Him as the hub. We can come together and find community only in in Him—as a family, as a church, as a global village. We do not put Christ in His central position; we can only acknowledge it, follow Him, and reap the blessings of unity that come from the station, He holds as Mediator, on earth as well as in heaven.[89]

The Mediator, Jesus Christ, has shown the way to practically recognize him in marital relationships. When spouses take the time to acknowledge the immediacy of Jesus and his standing between them, much of the weaknesses can be mitigated and the overflow of weaknesses into one another's lives can be minimized, and even prevented. Jesus takes the weaknesses and gives of his strength.

The way of Jesus

I refer to the way of Jesus as the gospel attitude. The gospel attitude is the way of Jesus that is found on a principle of engaging people before talking about their wrong (Romans 5:8; Matthew 1:21). Jesus loves sinners but hates sin. Therefore, wrongdoing does not prevent Jesus from engaging people. His

---

[88] Dietrich Bonhoeffer, *The Cost of Discipleship* (New York: The MacMillan Company, 1963), 108.

[89] Ron & Karen Flowers *Family Faith: experiencing love, contagious joy and Jesus at home* (Nampa, Idaho: Pacific Press Publishing Association, 2005), 86.

intention is always to bring out the best in people. Instead of being harsh and critical, Jesus displayed a gospel attitude that drew people to him instead of driving them away from him (Luke 15:1–2).

For instance, Jesus drew in a woman from Samaria with a gospel attitude. While it was shocking to find Jesus talking to a woman in the public in the middle of the day, it was even more radical to find Jesus talking to a Woman of Samaria. Noticeably, the scripture said of Jesus, "He needed to go through Samaria" (John 4:3–4). The Jews had no dealings with the Samaritans. So, Jews would have passed by Samaria because a long-standing feud existed between the Jews and Samaritans. The Jews refused to allow the Samaritans to participate in the building of the Temple in Jerusalem due to the fact that the Samaritans had inter-married with folk of the heathen culture and had a mixture of beliefs that differed from the Jews. Hence, they were not allowed to help build the Jerusalem Temple. They had their own Temple built on Mount Gerizim.

Nevertheless, Jesus went through Samaria and engaged a woman in a conversation. Jesus first referred to the topic of water. She was drawn in as she felt that a Jew should not be asking water of a Samaritan. But Jesus promised her water that would never run out. As she asked for the water, then Jesus told her to go and call her husbands. This shook her up, and she exclaimed, "I have no husband." Then Jesus said, "You answered correctly because you have had five husbands, and the one you have now is not your own." This revelation was enough to make her a believer and a missionary. Notice the gospel attitude of Jesus. He engaged the person first before addressing the wrongdoing.

In a marriage, couples need to acknowledge Jesus as the Mediator between them. Thus, when conflict arises, instead of a kneejerk reaction to criticize and point out the wrongdoing, the gospel attitude will naturally emerge. Don't go around or bypass the gospel attitude.

> When you need to show others their faults, do not talk down
> to them as though you are faultless and they are inferior to
> you. Instead talk with them as though you are standing side
> by side at the foot of the cross. Acknowledge your present on
> going need for the Savior. Admit ways that you have wrestled
> with the same or other sins or weaknesses, and give hope by

describing how God has forgiven you and currently working in you to help you change.[90.]

When Peter wrote his first epistle to the scattered pilgrims across the Roman Empire, he first began with the gospel attitude. He said,

> Praise be to the Lord God, and Father of our Lord Jesus Christ! In his great mercy he has given us new birth into a living hope through the resurrection of Jesus Christ from the dead, and into an inheritance that can never perish, spoil or fade—kept in heaven for you, who through faith are shielded by God's power until the coming of salvation that is ready to be revealed in the last time (1 Peter 1: 3–5).

After he pulled the flock in around Jesus, then he addressed holy living in the home, the church, and workplace.

> In Paul's letter to the Ephesians, he used the gospel attitude. He said, Praise to the God and Father of our Lord Jesus Christ, who has blessed us in the heavenly realms with every spiritual blessing in Christ. For he chose us in him before the creation of the world to be blameless and holy in his sight. In love he predestined us to be adopted as his sons through Jesus Christ in accordance with his pleasure and will—to the praise of his glorious grace, which he has freely given us in the one he loves. In him we have redemption through his blood and forgiveness sins, in accordance with the riches of God's grace that he lavished on us with all wisdom and understanding (Ephesians 1: 3–8).

After Paul engaged the believers and pulled them in through Jesus, he was in a good place to address oneness in the church, love and submission in marriage, submission in the workplace, parental authority in the home, spiritual growth, and spiritual warfare. If people are won, then it is easier to address conflict issues. The Gospel attitude validates people before addressing problems.

[90.] Ken Sande, *The Peace Maker* (Grand Rapids, MI: Baker Books, 2004), 172.

So, the antidote to self-righteousness is the righteousness of Christ. The gospel attitude shows that mercy wins over judgment (James 2:13). Also, all persons have weaknesses. Such acknowledgement requires humility.

> We are not all strong in all areas. Some are more susceptible to discouragement than others, or anger, or anxiety. Some struggle with physical weakness more than others. We all have some weakness in some area, or there would be no need for the power of God to operate in our lives.[91]

Demonstrating the Gospel attitude is more productive than focusing on weaknesses. The one who focuses on his spouse's weaknesses become judgmental and critical. This attitude puts the marriage on ice. The fact is that in many cases, the spouse that focuses on his wife's weaknesses does not see his own shortcomings (Matthew 7:1–5). Repentance allows spouses to change and see one another through the eyes the Mediator.

Repentance and the mind

A self-righteous pattern of behavior, such as judging, criticizing, condescending, and competing, has to be addressed first in the mind (James 4:1). A change in the mind would lead to a change in lifestyle. The word *metanoia* carries the idea of a change in the mind that lead to a change of life.[92] Moreover, "The word *metanoia* used in Acts 26:20, in its noun and verb forms refers to afterthought different from the former thought. It's biblical usage shows it to carry the idea of change in the mind resulting in altered conduct, which is a part of conversion (Romans 2:4; 2 Corinthians 2:9,10; Luke 15;7; Acts 2:38)."[93]

The goodness of God leads a person to repentance. A change takes place in the mind that turns one away from sinful pattern to godly lifestyle. In the case of marriage, the change in the mind turns a spouse away from negative thinking about her husband to a positive one. In this way, the spouse cooperates with God. As God works in the mind and the Holy Spirit transforms and

---

[91] Dave Harvey, *When Sinners Say I Do: Discovering The Power of The Gospel In Marriage* (Wapwallopen, PA: The Shepherd Press, 2007), 92.

[92] Jay E. Adams *The Christian Counselor's Manual: The Practice of Nouthetic Counseling* (Grand Rapids, MI: Zondervan, 1973), 173.

[93] T.H Jemison, *Christian Beliefs: Fundamental Biblical Teachings for Seventh-day Adventist College Classes* (Mountain View, CA: Pacific Press Publishing Association, 1959), 236.

renews the mind, the self-righteous spouse begins a lifestyle of replacing self-righteous habits with Christ-like habits. (Ephesians 4:17–34). While this process may be a struggle, it is possible to experience a change of mind that eventually alters conduct. The key is for each spouse to humbly cooperate with God and be obedient to his word. Jay E. Adams provides much-needed insights in the process of dehabituation and rehahabituation.[94]

According to Adams, the following elements of dehabituation and rehabituation are:

1. Becoming aware of the Practice (pattern) that must be dehabituated (put off);
2. Discover the Biblical alternative;
3. Structuring the whole situation for change;
4. Breaking links in the chain of sin;
5. Getting help from others;
6. Stressing the whole relationship with Christ;
7. Practicing the new pattern.

As God works in the mind, the husband and wife cooperate with God in a disciplined lifestyle. Change requires discipline within a secure structure. Through the Mediator Jesus, old habits will be put off and new habits will be put on. In this way, "I am right, and you are wrong" will be toppled.

❧

Discussion Questions

1. What makes self-righteousness such a problem in marital life?
2. How do we view the parable of the Pharisee and Tax Collector in the context of marriage relationship?
3. What is the significance of a reality with Jesus as Mediator?
4. Can you think of some reasons why a spouse would focus on the weaknesses of the other without being reflective?

---

[94] J. E Adams, *The Christian Counselor's Manual*

He uses Ephesians 4 to show the how wrong habits are put off and right habits are put on. He calls the process effecting biblical change. Life-dominating problems require discipline. 171–216

5. What is a Gospel attitude? What role does it play in marital relationships?

6. What is repentance? How does change take place in a self-righteous spouse?

7. How can you begin to practice the Gospel attitude?

8. What impact dehabituation (put off) and rehabituation (put on) could have on your marriage?

CHAPTER SEVEN

The tryrannous "I am free to do whatever I want."

"Your liberty to swing your arms ends where my nose begins."[95]

Self-fulfillment has become extremely toxic for marriages. Many married people seem to be more attune, in the way they live, to Abraham Maslow's hierarchy of needs than a desire to move closer to God. There seems to be a general acceptance, in certain quarters, that we are wanting creatures, and so we move invariantly from physiological needs, to safety needs, to social needs, to esteem needs and finally to self-actualization.[96] The challenge is that the felt needs of self-displace the ultimate need for God. So, in marriages, conflicts emerge due to the pursuit of self-fulfillment. While human beings were made to find fulfillment in surrender and an intimate relationship with God, there appears to be a reversal inward into self for fulfillment.

Looking about the welfare of self may not be an ignoble thing to do. However, God is best suited to bear the burdens of his children. Hence, looking for our welfare should be done within the context of our relationship with God, not an isolated pursuit of self-fulfillment. We live to glorify God,

---

[95] Stuart Chase, *Reader's Digest* "Vital Speeches of the Day" April, 1984, 153.

[96] Marlene Wilson, *How To Mobilze Church Volunteers* (Minneapolis, MA: Augsburg Publishing House, 1983), 36. Physiological needs are basic needs for food, water, air, shelter, etc. Safety need is to be safe and secure. Social need is to be liked, to affiliate with others, to belong. Esteem needs are to be recognized as a person of value and be appreciated. Self-actualization is to be the best we were meant to be.

not self (1 Corinthians 10:31). Self often thinks "one" and not "three," and therefore, self-fulfillment leads to marital tragedy. "Scripture is about dying to self, finding one's life by losing it, being crucified with Christ, and living only for Christ make it clear that realizing true fulfillment depends, not on preoccupation with fulfillment, but preoccupation with knowing God through absolute surrender."[97]

The thing is that there is much more reliance on securing and protecting the self by observing relational boundaries than building relationship with God. The secular approach to establishing boundaries are useful in many ways, but boundaries should not be a substitute for God. The very definition shows the usefulness of boundaries."Boundaries define us. They define what is me and what is not me. A boundary shows where I end and someone else and someone else begins, leading me to a sense of ownership."[98] In a sense, boundaries are fences that protect and secure persons in relationships. A boundary protects a spouse from spillovers of weaknesses from another spouse. In other words, due to clearly established boundaries, each person is aware of what is allowed and what is not allowed. While speaking the truth is allowed, verbal abuse, or any kind of abuse for that matter, is not allowed. Hence, in physical, emotional, and spiritual interactions, each person knows his or her responsibility. However, boundaries should be undergirded by a desire to glorify God and not simply to eliminate discomfort.

Only God can satisfy our souls. "A marriage will fail to be truly spiritually intimate if it moves in the direction of self. A successful marriage moves in the direction of obedience and relational surrender to God and increased relationship with the marriage partner."[99] While there is this move to establish boundaries to protect the self, many still encounter difficulties with relational boundaries. "Many people have good functional boundaries, but poor relational ones; that is, they can perform task at quite high level of competence, but they may not be able to tell a friend that they dislike their chronic lateness."[100] In the context of marriage, many spouses endure depression and

---

[97] Lawrence J. Crabb Jr., *The Marriage Builder* (Grand Rapids, MI: Zondervan, 1982), 10–11.

[98] Henry Cloud and John Townsend, *Boundaries: When to say Yes, When to say No To Take Control of Your Life*, (Grand Rapids, MI: Zondervan, 1992), 29.

[99] Steve and Valerie Bell, *Made To Be Loved: Enjoying Spiritual Intimacy with God and Your Spouse* (Chicago, IL: Moody Press, 1999), 36.

[100] Henry Cloud and John Townsend, *Boundaries: When To Say Yes When To Say No To Take Control of Your Life*, 60.

abuse because of fear that speaking the truth will end the marriage. Thus, simply saying no to abuse becomes an impossible task. This condition can change when the word of God becomes the interpretive grid for marital relationship and not self.

God and self in the context of boundaries

Relational boundaries are better established when human beings understand themselves in relation to God. Reinhold Niebuhr writes, "The second important characteristic of the Christian view of man is that he is understood primarily from the standpoint of God, rather than the uniqueness of his rational faculties or his relation to nature. He is made in the 'image of God.'"[101] God resourced human beings with reason and the capacity to develop personal relationship with God and their fellowmen (Genesis 1:26–28). Intimate association with God informs how human beings ought to relate to one another. Thus, a husband would bring his relationship with God to bear on his relationship with his wife. Spouses are accountable to God for the way they relate to one another. When God has his rightful place in the marriage, then the foundation for relational boundaries is established. In fact, the most important boundary has been established.

Human beings are unique and different from animals. In fact, reason and the capacity for relationship make marriage function efficiently in connection with God, not apart from God. Sadly, much of marital relationships today seem to be alienated from God. The consequences are dire. The Creation narrative shines light on this condition.

> Humans at creation are pictured as beings of love, goodness, trustworthiness, rationality and righteousness. It does not take a great deal of insight to realize that people are no longer completely lovely, good, responsible, rational, or righteous. Both human society at large and individual personal relationships are honeycombed with aggression, brutality and selfishness.[102]

---

[101] Reinhold Niebuhr, *The Nature and Destiny of Man* (New York: Charles Scribner's Sons, 1964), 13.

[102] George R. Knight, *Philosophy and Education: An Introduction in Christian Perspective* (Berrien Springs, MI: Andrews University Press, 1998), 193.

Human beings have experienced what is known biblically as the Fall (Genesis 3). Therefore, reconciliation with God through the Gospel of Jesus Christ is urgently needed for relational resource to love God and our fellowmen (Romans 5:1–5; Mark 12:30–31). In this way, marriages can be equipped to function in connection with God.

Too often people refuse to acknowledge that the failure of self is connected to the Fall. Thus, the answer to relational failure is sought from an unbiblical understanding of self.

> For years, educational experts, psychologists, and a growing number of Christian leaders have championed self-esteem as the panacea for all sorts of human miseries. According to the purveyors of this doctrine, if people feel good about themselves, they will behave better, have fewer emotional problems and achieve more. People, with high self-esteem we are told are less likely to commit crimes, act immorally, fail academically, or have problems in their relationships with others.[103]

In the 1990s, when relationships were being plagued by abuse, crime, divorce, and addiction, ninety percent of persons surveyed in a Gallup Poll indicated that they had healthy self-esteem.[104] Notice that while people were feeling good about themselves bad behaviors spiked.

When human beings are right with God and the radical sinfulness is addressed by the power of the Gospel, then human beings resist evil and learn to do well. This kind of peace with God motivates a spouse to do what makes for peace. One of Jesus's disciples must have had a good feeling about himself when he asked Jesus to command fire from heaven to fall and destroy the Samaritans. As the story went, Jesus and his disciples were in Samaria. The night had fallen, and they wanted a place to lodge for the night. The Samaritans refused to provide a lodging place. So, the vitriol came! "Lord do you want us to command fire to come down from heaven and consume them, just as Elijah did?" (Luke 9:54). This was the solution to the problem, as suggested by James and John—sons of thunder (Mark 3:17). Jesus rebuked

---

[103] John MacArthur, *Counseling: How To Counsel Biblically* (Nashville, TN: Thomas Nelson, 2005), 64.

[104] Jerry Adler et al., "Hey I'm Terrific," *Newsweek* (17 February 1992): 50.

them, and instead of engaging in destructive ways, demonstrated love. John was transformed in the presence of the love of Jesus and became the Apostle of love (1 John 1:1–4; 1 John 3:1; 1 John 4:7–11; 1 John 5:1–5).

When self is sacrificed for the cause of Christ, the love of Christ will motivate spouses to do acts of kindness to one another. Regardless of how one feels about himself, if the radical sinfulness is not addressed by power of the Gospel, then aggression, brutality, and selfishness will seamlessly come to the fore. The secular approach to establish boundaries to protect and improve self is not sufficient. "The setting of boundaries to prevent possible use or abuse often leads to self-centered, arrogant, autonomous self-protection."[105]. This is why God has revealed himself as the relational God. He shows us how to relate to one another in love. God is our boundary (1 John 4: 7–21).

Incommunicable and communicable attributes of God

God made human beings with the capacity to think. Thinking has more to do with relationships than many may be willing to acknowledge. In fact, what a person thinks about God determines his or her perspective of God and relationship with God. One who thinks of God as despotic and arbitrary may not move close to God. The person who thinks of God as loving may see a prize opportunity to draw close to God. "What you think about God shapes your whole relationship with him. In addition what you believe God thinks about you determines how close you will go towards him."[106]. A. W Tozer declares, "We tend by a secret law of the soul to move toward our mental image of God."[107]. One of the productive ways to think about God is by examining his attributes. God's attributes comprise sufficient material to focus on for forming a mental image that draws one close to God.

The incommunicable attributes are the natural qualities of God that make God distinctly separate from human beings. The qualities make God, God. T.H. Jemison provides a list of incommunicable attributes. They are eternity, omnipresence, omniscience, omnipotence, and immutability.[108]. God, who is

---

[105] Samuel Beckett, *Waiting for Godot* (New York: Grove, 1954), 32.

[106] Chip Ingram, *God As He Longs For You To See Him* (Grand Rapids, MI: Baker Books, 2004), 20.

[107] A. W Tozer, *The knowledge of The Holy* (New York: HarperCollins, 1961), 1.

[108] T. H. Jemison, *Christian Beliefs* (Mountain View, CA: Pacific Press Publishing Association, 1959), 75–76 Eternity means God has no beginning and no ending (Exodus 3:14; Psalm 90:2; Revelation 1:8). Omnipresence means that God has a spiritual presence everywhere, fully at the same time (Psalm 139:7–12; Jerimiah 23:23–24; Hebrews 4:13; Acts 17:27–28). Omniscience means that

God all by himself, has shared with us his moral attributes. So, God is not distant but personal. Also, he has shared with us his relational qualities. These are the communicable attributes of God. T.H. Jemison lists them as Holiness (Psalm 99:9), Righteousness (Ezra 9:15), Justice (Revelation 22:12), Mercy (Isaiah 55:7), Loving-kindness (Jerimiah 31:3; Graciousness (Titus 2:11), Truth (1John 5:20), Purity (Habakkuk 1:13), Love (1 John 4:8).

An accurate knowledge of God is needed for a relationship with God that overflows into relationship with your spouse. "When you have an accurate view of God, you understand that he is all-knowing, all-seeing, all-powerful, and thoroughly good. He is for you. You can have difficulties, but you are not uptight and you're not anxious and you're not worrying because your life is under his care."[109.] When married couples think about God in this way, they will move close to God. As couples move close to God, they move close to one another. Love replaces fear, while goodness and mercy replace evil. A relationship with God, founded on an accurate knowledge and view of God, reminds couples that all their needs are met in God. So, when they err, they seek God to restore them to a place where they could love and respect one another.

Love and Respect

When a husband and wife experience a close relationship with God through Jesus Christ, love and respect will mutually overflow into each spouse. Both should be willing to be vulnerable and receive and give love and respect. There should be no hidden agenda.

> It is in the context of nakedness that the biblical roles of husbands and wives in marriage must be considered. Both Paul and Peter delineate the roles of both mates in the marriage relationship. Husbands are clearly called to love their wives as Christ loved the church and gave himself for her. Wives are called to submit to their husbands as the church submits to the

---

God has perfect knowledge of himself, human beings, everything in creation, past, present and future, and knows the best ways to accomplish his purpose (Job 37:16; Psalm 139:2-4; Isaiah 46:9-10; 48:5-8). Omnipotence means that God is able to his will, and none can stand in the way of God achieving his purpose (Jerimiah 32:17; Genesis 1:1-3; Daniel 4:17, 25, 35; Matthew 19:26; Revelation 19:6). Immutability means that God is unchangeable. He is perfect and cannot get better than perfect or worse than perfect (Malachi 3:6; Psalm 33:11; James 1:17).

[109.] Chip Ingram, *God As He Longs for You To See Him.* 244

leadership of Christ in the church. Both of these pictures require authentic vulnerability before the other.[110.]

A reading of Ephesians chapter five shows the model relationship between Jesus and the Church. What submission could be more profound than that of Christ dying for the church (Philippians 2:5–8)? This is servant leadership motivated by love. Just as it is true that the way we think about God determines our trajectory towards or away from God, so also the way a man or a woman thinks about one another or views one another determines distance or proximity to one another. If a wife has a mental image of her husband as a good, just, sacrificial, and loving person, a Christian wife will not see submission as subjugation and slavery but intimacy. When a husband thinks of his wife as one who should be nourished and cherished as his own body, he will respect her (Ephesians 5:21–33).

Love and respect are two sides of the same coin. The marriage coin has love on one side and respect on the other. Nonetheless, it is essentially one coin. The issue of sacrificial leadership on the part of the man and submission on the part of the woman should not become a political football because of modern liberalism, women's movements, and rabid individualism. The context of mutuality supports roles motivated by love and respect. These are healthy boundaries in marital relationship. Hence, both are free to serve one another in sacrificial leadership and submission. No one is free to do whatever he wants. Our freedom exists within boundaries (Exodus 20:1–17; John 3:16).

Discussion Questions

1. Why felt needs seem to displace the ultimate need for God? Describe the various needs of wanting creatures? Is it a meaningful discipline to die to self?

2. What is the essence of a secular pursuit of boundaries? What questions does this raise about how God fits in the whole discussion about boundaries?

[110.] Michael and Michelle Anthony, *A Theology for Family Ministries*, (Nashville, TN: B&H Academic, 2011), 113.

3. What is the significance of God as a boundary?

4. What is unique about the attributes of God in the context of boundaries?

5. What is the meaning of boundaries?

6. What is the understanding of love and respect in marriage?

7. Do you experience conflict between sacrificial leadership and submission in your marriage?

Chapter Eight

The tryrannous "I can say whatever I want to say."

If it is possible, as far as it depends on you, live at peace with everyone. —Romans 12:18

When love and respect dissipate in a marriage, invariably, the tongue loses its mooring. An uncontrollable tongue sets fires that destroy relationships. In the absence of love and respect, the tongue is fuelled by anger, hurt, frustration, fear, guilt, and self-centeredness. Therefore, torrents of hurting words issue out of mates' mouths instead of healing words. Persons who are hurt and angry hurt others. In such a state, couples rail against one another as a matter of course and become desensitized to the adverse effects and wounds caused by their words. Eventually, what seems like openness and transparency soon becomes a fire that threatens the existence of the marriage.

Fires can be absolutely destructive. As I write this book, fires are raging in California and leaving vast destruction of historic proportion in their path. Many believe it is the result of climate change. In like manner, the climate in marriage can change. In fact, the climate does change when love and respect wane, thus allowing the tongue to become ungovernable. In the absence of control, it ignites fires that cause inestimable hurt to spouses. Such hurt may never be healed.

Climate change in marital relationship allows the tongue to target the weaknesses of spouses. In the forest, the dry shrubs and leaves on the forest floor could easily ignite into huge conflagration. So also, people have weaknesses that could become ignited and compromise the integrity of the marriage. When these weaknesses are assaulted, the result is a destructive pattern of communication. Markman, Stanley, and Blumberg refer to a destructive pattern as Escalation, Invalidation, Negative Interpretation, and Withdrawal and Avoidance.[111] Escalation can be like a forest fire. Couples begin to respond negatively to each other and upping the ante of negative exchange. Behind the words are anger, frustration, and contempt for one another. Instead of hearing one another out, they are hurting one another. As compulsiveness takes over, words may be said that threaten the very existence of the marriage. In fact, even intimate knowledge may be used as weapon to hit below the belt. The fire rages as large portion of intimacy is destroyed creating extreme distance and making the future very grim.

Invalidation continues the blazing fire. In subtle ways and sarcasm, couples put down one another and invalidate character, thoughts, and feelings. Due to the fact that love and respect have been replaced by anger, frustration, hurt, self-centeredness, no one respects or acknowledges the viewpoints of each other. The putdowns and name-calling destroy the massive territory of trust built up over a long time. Couples use words that could burn the marriage down to the ground.

Negative interpretation is more fuel for the fire. Based on the bad experiences of the past, couples impute negative motives to each other in a consistent manner. Thus, even though there may be positive things about the marriage, they are not recognized. Character is attacked, and any good done is not recognized as genuine. They may see one another as liars and, thus, treat each other that way.

Withdrawal and avoidance may be an effort to get out of the fire, but that may be futile. A spouse may withdraw or walk out, shutdown during the exchange. Another mate may avoid or try to stop the conversation all together. In reality, one mate pursues, and the other withdraws. The one who withdraws sees the pursuer as aggressive and insensitive. The one who pursues sees the withdrawer as uncaring and self-centered.

All this is a result of climate change in the marriage. Love and respect have been replaced by anger, fear, guilt, frustration, and self-centeredness. "For

---

[111] Howard J. Markman, Scott M. Stanley, Susan L. Blumberg *Fighting For Your Marriage* (San Francisco, CA: Jossey-Bass, 2001), 43–61.

out of the heart come evil thoughts, murder, adultery, sexual immorality, theft, false testimony, slander (Matthew 15:19)." James writes, "What causes fights and quarrels among you? Don't they come your desires that battle within you" (James 4:1). Writing specifically about the tongue, James writes,

> Likewise the tongue is a small part of the body, but it makes great boasts. Consider what a great forest is set on fire by a small spark. The tongue also is a fire, a world of evil among the parts of the body. It corrupts the whole person, sets the whole course of his life on fire, and is it self set on fire by hell… With the tongue we praise our Lord and Father, and with it we curse men who have been made in God's likeness. Out of the same mouth come praise and cursing. My brothers this should not be (James 3:5–10).

Many lives and marriages have been set on fire by the tongue and have been reduced to a distant specter of the original state.

Martha Peace puts it poignantly,

> What we say and how we say it can hurt others. Words can crush and pierce people. Some wounds may never heal. In marriages husbands and wives have the potential to hurt each other deeply by the words they say. Often couples communicate in unbiblical and ungodly ways. Instead of love and kindness there is strife, anger and malice. Instead of wisdom there is foolishness. Instead of careful words there are careless words.[112]

If marriages would survive such a harsh climate has to be addressed.

Addressing climate change in the marriage

"Out of the same mouth come praise and cursing. My brothers this should not be" (James 3:10). When the Holy Spirit changes the mind, the same Holy Spirit pours the love of God in the heart (Romans 5:5). The Holy Spirit provides power to decide on the right way to use the tongue (Zechariah 4:6). Instead of using the tongue to inflame the weaknesses in one another, couples

[112] Martha Peace *The Excellent Wife* (Minnesota: Focus Publishing INC., 2005), 187.

can choose to talk about the positive qualities of one another. In this way, a positive image of your spouse is formed in the mind. A mate gravitates towards a spouse whose image is positive in his mind. In other words, spouses become attractive to each other again (Genesis 2:24–25). "By simply reminding yourself of your spouse's positive qualities—you can prevent a happy marriage from deteriorating. The simple reason is that fondness and admiration are antidotes to contempt."[113]

How is the environment in your marriage? Is it debilitating or healing? Is it spiritual or secular? The use of the environment as a metaphor helps couples to see more clearly dynamics that affect the climate and how they influence the tone of the marriage. So, couples need to diagnose their own marriages from time to time to see where improvement is needed in the environment. Marriages are dying for want of the oxygen of love and respect. Asphyxiation is the condition when fire takes the oxygen away, and so, people suffocate or die for want of oxygen. Attention has to be paid to the marriage environment. Checking on the marriage environment prevents destructive fires. In other words, issues in relationships could be addressed early before they become inflammatory. One of the ways to do that is to periodically do a marriage environment questionnaire. [114]

A marriage environment questionnaire
1. What is the environment like in your marriage?
2. Do you see any changes in the environment, and are there warning signs before the changes?
3. How comfortable is it in your marriage? How comfortable is it for your spouse in his/her role and life? Do you need to wear protective gear?
4. Do you do the forecasting of changes in the environment or you depend on the experts?
5. Are there different areas of the marriage that have different environment? Who could be found in those areas?
6. Can couples and ideas grow in the environment? Or die?

---

[113] John Gottman, *The Seven Principles of Making Marriage Work* (New York: Three Rivers Press, 1999), 65.

[114] Fritz Steele/Stephen Jenks, *The Feel of the Work Place* (Massachusetts: Addison-Wesley, 1977), 177–178. I revised the questionnaire to suit the marriage environment. Their questionnaire addressed climate in the workplace. On the contrary, I revised sentences to adequately address the environment that give rise to climate in the marriage.

7. Who is responsible to do something or talk about the environment?
8. Who provides energy in this marriage, and where are they located?
9. Is there sufficient safety for one to breathe or express his or herself emotionally?
10. Is there enough challenge for couples to grow?

The results provide enough information for couples to prepare for any inclemency in the weather. A number of proactive measures are at the disposal of couples in redirecting the tongue for positive use. First, use the tongue to minister hope to your spouse (Proverbs 12:18; 18:21). Second, take on a servant attitude.

> Taking on this servant attitude over the long hall will create sanctuary in a home and marriage. Essentially, it entails seeing your mate as your primary ministry day after day. It means seeing your spouse through God's eyes; as someone who is precious, someone he has made to be loved and given to your care as the primary human instrument through whom His love is experienced.[115]

This kind of attitude become expressive in words of healing and grace.

Third, choose to go the way of positive interpretation instead of negative interpretation (1 Corinthians 13:6–7). Negative feelings should not trump facts. Fourth, speak the truth in love (Ephesians 4:15; Romans 12:14). In many cases, the way we begin a conversation will determine the direction of the exchange. If we begin with love, the chance of the exchange being productive is high (1 Thessalonians 5:14–15). Fifth, choose to speak as team members and not competitors. Sixth, choose to examine the motives of your heart before pouring our words (James 4:1–3; Matthew 15:19). Seventh, treat sensitive matters with utmost care. Make wise choices of time and place to talk about sensitive issues in person (Ecclesiastes 3:1). Eighth, choose to show your spouse love and respect before talking about wrongdoing (Luke 10:25–37). Ninth, choose the rigor of talking clearly about a matter so that there would be no misunderstanding. "Therefore, whenever you need to communicate important

---

[115] Steve and Valerie Bell, *Made To Be Loved: Enjoying Spiritual Intimacy with God and Your Spouse*(Chicago, IL: Moody Press, 1999), 90.

information, think carefully about your words and look for words and look for ways that they might be vague, imprecise, or potentially misleading. As you tighten up what you say, you can prevent many of the misunderstandings that fuel conflict."[116]

The responsibility rests on both spouses to engage in these fire prevention measures. They will keep the marital environment in a healthy state so that should a fire get started, mitigating measures are in place. In fact, observable signs will point to the possibility of climate change. Hence, couples can work together to restore the environment. Words can heal as well as hurt; therefore, words should be used responsibly and with a sense of accountability to one another and to God. This is proactive measure against "I can say whatever I want to say."

❦

Discussion Questions

1. How do you view the tongue in your marriage? What is it like? How is it used?
2. Trace the way the tongue could become unruly and affect the existence of your marriage.
3. What is the benefit of using the metaphor of environment to describe the magnitude of marital climate change?
4. What is the result of your marriage environment questionnaire? How do you plan to respond to the result?
5. What does it mean to be responsible for your words?
6. How can you change from negative use of the tongue to positive use of the tongue?.
7. Reflect on a destructive pattern of communication. How can you avoid it?

---

[116] Ken Sande, *The Peace Maker: A Biblical Guide to Resolving Personal Conflict* (Grand Rapids, MI: Baker House, 2004), 176.

Chapter Nine

The tryrannous "I want it! I don't have the money, but I must have it."

Money is a terrible master but an excellent servant.—P. T. Barnum, 1810-1891, Founder of Barnum and Bailey Circus

In marriage, money never ceases to be a matter of concern. "Most of the research on marital conflict reveals that there are three main issues that married couples consistently fight about: money, sex and communication."[117] It is not difficult to see money popping up at every point of the life cycle, as it is deeply connected to safety and security in marriages. Robert Blood points out, "Where as in law problems are concentrated at the beginning of marriage, and child rearing problems in the middle, financial conflict spread over the whole life cycle, taking new forms as circumstances change."[118] Many marriages seem to be colonized by deficit spending. Consumer items are producing mountain of debt. Yet many couples continue to be colonized by credit buying. It seems to be ingrained in the mind. In fact, many couples go as far as borrowing large sums of money from lending institutions to pay for wedding expenses. What drives this behavior is incorrect thinking.

Deficit spending is now accepted as a normal way of life. In spite of the pain the family suffers, the trend of economic theories is reinforcing the

---

[117] Bryan Craig, *Searching for Intimacy in Marriage* p. 132.

[118] Robert O. Blood, *Marriage, Second Edition* (New York: The Free Press, 1969), 234.

acceptability of credit buying. The government, as well as lending institutions, is in favor of deficit spending. In fact, there are many attractive credit cards that reinforce the culture of credit buying. Burkett states, "The increase incidence of divorce is a direct result of too much debt. Nearly 80 percent of divorced couples between the ages of 20 and 30 state that financial problems were the primary cause of their divorce."[119]

In spite of the corporate acceptability of deficit spending, couples should make informed choices to take control of their lives. The consequences of debt, resulting from a culture of credit buying, are too painful for working-class families.

A change of attitude

The mental tendency to love debt should change. Couples should decide in their minds that debt is not acceptable. Then proceed to make lifestyle changes. Richard A. Swenson suggests the following:

1. Live within your harvest. Contentment and simplicity will help in this regard.
2. Decrease spending.
3. Increase income. Decreasing spending and managing the surplus with maximum effectiveness could do this.
4. Increase savings. One increases savings not for protection but for provision.
5. Make a budget.
6. Discard credit cards. Pay cash for purchases.
7. Resist impulsive spending.
8. Emphasize usefulness over fashion.
9. Use it up. Wear it out. Make it do. Do without.
10. Put God's kingdom first.[120]

Burkett points out, "Regardless of how it seems today, debt is not normal in any economy and should not be normal for God's people. We live in a debt-ridden society that is now virtually dependent on a constant expansion of credit

---

[119] Larry Burkett, *Debt Free Living* (Chicago, IL: Moody Press, 1999), 16.

[120] Richard A. Swenson, *Margin: Restoring Emotional, Physical, Financial, and Time Reserves to Overloaded Lives* (Colorado Springs, CO: Nav Press, 1995), 178–172.

to keep the economy going. This is a symptom of a society no longer willing to follow God's direction."[121.] A change in attitude and mind is needed to break the love affair between married couples and debt. Selfish desires need to be surrendered to the Word of God.

A plan of action

In order to liquidate existing debt, couples should have a plan. A change of attitude will be an asset in the activation of the plan. A written plan of action in the form of a budget should suffice as a step forward. This plan will affect the lifestyle of couples. Take a look at the recommended budget on an income of two thousand dollars net.

Recommended	The DeSilver's Budget
Tithe.... $200.00	Tithe...$200.00
Housing....$ 550.00	Housing....$900.00
Auto....$200.00	Auto...$250.00
Food....$250.00	Food ...$260.00
Clothing...$85.00	Clothing... $90.00
Medical.... $80.00	Medical...$00.00
Insurance....$85.00	Insurance....$0.00
Entertainment....$90.00	Entertainment...$50.00
Miscellaneous....$80.00	Miscellaneous.... $50.00
Savings...$85.00	Savings.....$0.00
Debt...$85.00	Debt....$300.00
Education...$100.00	Education..... $50.00
TOTAL: $1890.00	TOTAL: $2150.00
A lifestyle change results in a wiser dispersion of funds. This is about living within your harvest.	

[121.] Larry Burkett, *Debt Free Living* (Chicago: Moody Press, 1999), 57.

A lifestyle change, such as decreasing housing costs, helped the DeSilivers to reduce their debt significantly. A plan of action in the form of a written budget can break the love affair with debt.[122.] However, in that plan, couples should have goals to get out of debt. Every family should set its own goals for getting out of debt. Goals should be specific, measurable, and realistic. Moreover, they should be based on sound principles and values. Each person should acknowledge the role his or her has to play in order to achieve the goals.

Goals should be compartmentalized into immediate goals, intermediate goals, and ultimate goals. In order to achieve the ultimate goal, which is freedom from debt, there is need for discipline and self-control. When the ultimate goal is achieved the couple should guard against slipping back into debt. This is why a change of thinking and attitude is so critical. Couples can buttress their attitude, going forward with guardrails. These are a mission statement, saving strategy, and the question of ownership.

Mission Statement

Without a mission statement, the society is allowed to force itself on the family, causing the family to react. The reactive measures put a strain on the family. One of the ways to take control and be proactive is by having a family mission statement. Swenson said, "The spontaneous tendency of our culture is to inexorably add details to our lives… We must deal with more things per person than at any other time in history. Yet one can comfortably handle only so many details in his or her life."[123.] How do you respond to one more purchase, one more debt, one more expectation, and one more commitment? A mission statement could be helpful.

"The mission statement becomes its constitution, the standard, the criterion for evaluation and decision making. It gives continuity and unity to the family as well as direction. When individual's values are harmonized with those of the family, members work together for common purposes that are deeply felt."[124.]

Moreover, Covey points out,

[122.] Larry Burkett, Debt-free Living p.111-117

[123.] Richard A. Swenson, *Margin* 74.

[124.] Steven Covey, *The 7 Habits of Highly Effective People* 138

The mission statement becomes a framework for thinking, for governing the family. When the problems and crises come, the constitution is there to remind the family members of the things that matter most and provide direction for problem solving and decision making based on correct principles.[125]

A mission statement lends itself to the kind of governance that will keep a couple out of debt.

Saving Strategies

"Dishonest money dwindles away, but he who gathers money little by little makes it grow."[126] Ray Linder contends, "Saving money is the corner stone of personal finance."[127] Saving should be a priority. Saving, however small or large, should be consistent and regular. Saving is not hoarding: saving is for provision. Linder suggests three steps in a saving plan:

1. Pay God first.
2. Pay yourself next by determining the appropriate saving level
3. Spend the rest on bills and yourself.[128]

"In the house of the wise are stores of choice food and oil, but a foolish man devours all he has."[129] It is true that a dollar saved can be put to many uses, but a dollar spent is gone forever.

The ownership questions

"Closely tied to God's provision is God's ownership.... In the Bible, however, God's absolute rights as owner and our relative right as stewards are unmistakably clear."[130] Take a look at the following scriptural references:

---

[125] Ibid., 138.

[126] Proverbs 13:11

[127] Ray Linder, *Making The Most of Your Money* (Illinois: Zondervan Publishing House, 1995), 81.

[128] Ibid., 88

[129] Proverbs 21:20.

[130] Richard L. Foster, *Money, Sex and Power* (New York: Harper and Row Publishers Inc. 1989), 41.

"Whatever is under the whole heaven is mine" (Job 41:11). "All the earth is mine" (Exodus 19:5–6). "The earth is the Lord's and the fullness thereof" (Psalm 24:1).

Couples need to settle the question of ownership and see their responsibility as managers. The innate selfishness of man is the reason for not accepting God's ownership. This has resulted in giving property rights the ascendency over human rights. God is the absolute owner. He demands a fair and equitable distribution of wealth among all people (Deuteronomy 14:28,29; Exodus 23:11; Leviticus 25:23). Accepting God's ownership of everything liberates us from a possessive and anxious spirit. (Philippians 4:4–9).

There is need for couples to take personal responsibility for debt reduction, avoidance, and liquidation. Albeit national trends influence individual behavior, one must choose not to get involved in consumer credit, which is a one-way ticket to debt. Debt upsets the balance in the family. It brings about unwanted tension, which results in miscommunication and family breakdown. The price is too high. Consequently, there should be a personal financial strategy to keep the family debt-free. A couple lives under tyranny when the spouses are actuated by "I want it! I don't have the money! But I must have it!"

Discussion Questions

1. How does money affect the family cycle?
2. How does this chapter affect your view of debt?
3. What role does the society and institutions play in consumer credit?
4. How does the Bible approach the issue of money management?
5. What is the value of having a budget and goals? Explain the importance of a mission statement, saving strategy, and ownership.
6. How can a person have a change of attitude toward deficit spending?

CHAPTER TEN

The tryrannous "I don't feel like I am in love anymore."

With somebody to love even the most severely afflicted can make it.—Ken Duckworth

The Christian marriage is permanent. However, it is not an endless romance of living happily ever after. Marriage necessitates growth and change, and such an experience includes discomfort. For many couples, it appears as though they forget the promise to stay together for better or for worse, for richer or for poorer. The matter of growth and change in marriage falls within the experience of sanctification. Becoming one flesh could be a sanctifying process. Some experiences may be comfortable, while other experiences could be uncomfortable.

It is of grave importance that couples do not lose their relationship with God in the marriage. Should they compromise their intimate association with God, a door opens for feeling to dominate the marriage. This is one reason "that Christians ought to choose partners that share their beliefs and value system. More generally it could be said that God's people are to avoid partnerships that compromise their faith and integrity as Christians."[131] The matter of faith being developed on the inside by the Holy Spirit makes couples strong to adequately deal with wacky emotions.

---

[131] David Peterson, *Possessed by God: A New Testament Theology of Sanctification and Holiness* (Downers Grove, IL: InterVarsity Press, 1995), 87. Peterson commented on 1 Corinthians 7:12–16,39. Even in mixed marriages, the believing spouse sanctifies the unbelieving spouse. The unbelieving spouse is presented with an opportunity to respect God.

Couples could actually feel that they are no longer "in love." This is a powerful force that could only be countered by an abiding intimacy with God. Is it any wonder that Paul admonishes men to love their wives as Christ loved the Church? Is it any wonder that Paul admonishes women to submit to their husbands as unto the Lord (Ephesians 5:21–33)? The relationship with the Lord should be paramount, as this is a fortress against building a marriage on feeling. The feeling of "being in love" is a good thing but it is not primary.

> What is called being in love is a glorious state, and in several ways good for us. It helps to make us generous and courageous, it opens our eyes not only to the beauty of the beloved but to all beauty, and it subordinates (especially at first) our mere animal sensuality; in that sense love is the great conqueror of lust. No one in his senses would deny that being in love is far better than either common sensuality or cold self-centeredness. But as I said before "the most dangerous thing you can do is to take any one impulse of your own and set it up as the thing you should follow at any cost." Being in love is a good thing but it's not the best thing.[132]

While this feeling of "being in love" doesn't last, it doesn't mean that one has to stop loving. In such moments, God provides the motivation needed to love when one doesn't feel like being in love (2 Corinthians 5:14). In fact, Love is deep, not surface and whimsical.

> It is a deep unity maintained by the will and deliberately strengthened by habit; reinforced by (in Christian marriages) the grace which both partners asked and received from God. They can have this love for each other even at those moments when they don't like each other; as you love yourself when you don't like yourself[133]

---

[132] C. S. Lewis, *Mere Christianity* (San Francisco, CA: HarperCollins Publishers, 2001), 108.

[133] Ibid., 109

When the aura of romance and "being in love" wanes and fluctuates, some couples may feel that they are not compatible, so they should separate. Actually, this is an opportunity for growth and development.

When couples wrestle with discomfort, together, with the help of God, they become stronger and eventually love one another with a deeper intensity. God works with couples through the feeling of not "being in love." He does so sometimes in strange ways.

> Our romantic dream is of a couple walking off into the sunset living happily ever after. But God designs us so that by our encounter we will be unable to congratulate ourselves that we are all right and have to face what is in us. We are lazy and unwilling to see the truth. We "hide from our own flesh" (Isaiah 58:7). Therefore God gives us "beloved enemy." Peace is not always God's design.[134]

It must be seen for what it is; God is working out our sanctification. The natural feeling of not "being in love" is an opportunity to continue to love. If couples continue to love through the pain, the feeling will return after the pain. "No discipline seems pleasant at the time, but painful. Later on however it produces a harvest of righteousness and peace, for those who have been trained by it (Hebrews 12:11)."

The protective habits of love
If the physical relationship is going to last, love has to be protected. While reinforcement comes from God, couples should develop habits that protect physical connectedness. In this way, couples cooperate with the Holy Spirit. It may take about three weeks to develop a habit, and another three weeks to make it second nature. The unfortunate thing is that many couples develop habits in the marriage that become a pattern of life which cause couples to become estranged from one another. They have been in the gym of life training themselves in patterns that destroy intimacy, without paying attention. The Apostle Peter explains the process.

---

[134] John & Paula Sandford, *Restoring The Christian Family* (Tulsa, OK: Victory House INC., 1979), 55

In 2 Peter 2:14, Peter speaks about people whose hearts are "*trained* in greed." Trained is the same word Paul used (*gymnazo*), the word from which gymnastic comes. A heart that has been exercised in greed is one that has faithfully practiced greed so that greediness has become natural.[135]

Therefore, once a couple can self-examine and discover the habits that promote alienation instead of connectedness, then they are in a position to replace these habits with those that encourage closeness. Without paying attention, couples may develop some habits that undermine their physical relationship. There are a few habits that couples should watch out for and replace them, should they arise. Les and Leslie Parrott refer to bad things that happen to good marriage. In their treatment of the bad things, the habits are readily seen.

1. The habit of putting work before the marriage. Hence, couples may spend more time with work-related matters than marital interaction and togetherness. Interestingly, while many value marriage and family over work, more time is given to work than family life.[136]

2. The habit of becoming dismissive and taking one another for granted. Getting chores done and bills paid become substitute for uplifting conversations.

3. The habit of giving up on recreational interests and depends on the marriage to bring daily excitement. For example, instead of couples engage in biking together, the one who likes biking may simply abandon that interest because the other partner is not interested.

4. The habit of drifting. Les and Leslie Parrott write, "Most couples who drift apart still care deeply for one another. The only problem is that they now feel so different. You don't have to allow the increasing gap between you and your partner to go any wider. You have the power to pull it together and enjoy meaningful connections with your partner in areas of your life you may have thought your partner would never share."[137]

---

[135] Jay E. Adams *The Christian Counselor's Manual: The Practice of Nouthetic Counseling* (Grand Rapids, MI: Zondervan, 1973), 182.

[136] Alain Sanders, "Jobs vs. Family," *Time* (December 13, 1999): 63.

[137] Les and Leslie Parrott *When Bad Things Happen To Good Marriages: How To Stay Together When Life Pulls You Apart,* (Grand Rapids, MI: Zondervan Publishing House, 2001), 98. The authors

5.   The habit of irresponsible consumer spending and credit buying. Debt puts a strain on the marriage and could foster a negative mood in the relationship.

6.   The habit of being secretive. Marriage requires self-disclosure on matters pertaining to the unity of couples. The habit of keeping secrets from one another could sap the feeling of being in love. An undisclosed secret could be a hurt in the past. The hurt in the past could be fodder for negative thinking.

It is important that these habits be replaced, or the physical relationship could be threatened. When there is no feeling of "being in love," then "lovemaking" will be adversely affected. The question is, what habits could replace the aforementioned ones?

Habits replacement

When a couple identifies the habits that need replacement, partners should team up and decide to make changes with the help of God. Some habits may require the expertise of a counselor. However, in many cases, couples could work together and hold one another accountable for habit replacement. This is the work of putting off what is not good and putting on what is good (Ephesians 4:20–32). For instance, if couple is estranged because more time is spent on work-related matters than family togetherness, then both spouses can reorganize work activities so that more time is spent with one another than with work.

Habit replacement involves a divine and human effort. Therefore, couples should learn to develop discipline in obedience to the word of God and prayer. The power behind lasting change for good is the Holy Spirit.

It is not effort apart from the Holy Spirit that produces godliness. Rather, it is through the power of the Holy Spirit alone that one can endure. Of his own effort a man may persist in learning to skate, but he will not persist in pursuit of godliness. A Christian does good works because the Spirit first works in him.[138]

---

write about some bad things that creep up on marriage. These are busyness, irritability, boredom, drifting, debt, and past pain.

[138] Jay E. Adams *The Christian Counselors Manual*, 186.

Take note that as a couple moves towards God, they are in a better position to cultivate new habits that are sustainable which bring them closer together.

Habits that keep couples in proximity to one another create an environment for human sensuality and romance. Thus, the relationship has a climate that fosters the feeling of "being in love," which enhances "making love." The good habits are like coals in the fire. "The fires of love burn very easily: it's what couples do with the embers that count most! To have your love and passion last a lifetime, you both have to tend the coals from which future fires spring. You have to protect sensual and sexual life, nurture it, and above all, make it a priority."[139]

Couples who experience low sexual desires will see a marked uptick in their desires when unifying habits are practiced. Mutual reading of scripture, praying together, worshiping together, cuddling together, walking together, exercising together, bathing together, eating together, having fun together, talking together, mutual touching and sharing of appreciation, sharing gifts with one another, writing love notes to one another, discussing feelings and sexual preferences, resting well and eating well are like coals that keep new fires of love burning. These are coals or habits that should be protected at all cost.

Markman, Stanley, and Blumberg point out,

> We don't believe that couples fall out of love as much as they fail to protect and preserve their love by investing in and nourishing their relationship on a daily basis. The major reason attraction and passion ebb is that couples neglect the very things that build and maintain attraction in the first place—friendship, fun, sensuality and sexuality. So the best lovers are in a sense fun lovers.[140]

Therefore, the habits that tend not protect and preserve love should be replaced by the ones which protect and preserve love. Couples, with the help of the Holy Spirit, should be daily in the gym of life, with the help of the Holy Spirit, developing robust habits that become natural patterns, which ignite passion and sustain love.

---

[139] Howard J. Markman, Scott M. Stanley, Susan L. Blumberg, *Fighting for Your Marriage* (San Francisco, CA: Jossey-Bass, 2001), 248.

[140] Howard J. Markman, Scott M. Stanley, Susan L. Blumberg *Fighting For Your Marriage*, 243.

Biblical admonition

The marital union is intended to bring joy to your spouse. Self-gratification, in any form, robs the union of joy and intimacy. Many times self-gratification takes advantage of the physical relationship. Physical relationship should be all about a ministry to one another in marriage. However, such ministry should be done out of a love relationship with God. A husband's love for God determines his love for his wife and the direction of the marriage.

> When I have learnt to love God better than my earthly dearest, I shall love my earthly dearest better than I do now. In so far as I learn to love my earthly dearest at the expense of God and instead of God, I shall be moving towards the state in which I shall not love my earthly dearest at all. When first things are put first, second things are not suppressed but increased."[141]

Often, like a thief, self-gratification comes in and turns the marriage into an arid wilderness of war. This is why spouses should have deep spiritual intimacy with God, which equips them to love one another. Love does not seek its own gratification but the joy of the other (1 Corinthians 13:4–8).

In the arena of sexuality in marriage, the Bible support other-centeredness as opposed to self-gratification.

> The husband should fulfill his marital duty to his wife, and likewise the wife to her husband (1 Corinthians 7:3).

> May your fountain be blessed, and may you rejoice in the wife of your youth. A loving doe, a graceful deer—may her breasts satisfy you always, may you ever be captivated by her love" (Proverbs 5:18–19).

> Enjoy life with your wife, whom you love, all the days of this meaningless life that God has given you under the sun—all your meaningless days. For this is your lot in life and in your toilsome labor under the sun" (Ecclesiastes 9:9). Do not

---

[141] C.S Lewis, as quoted in Wayne Martindale and Jerry Root, *The Quotable Lewis* (Wheaton, ILL: Tyndale, 1989), 411.

deprive each other except by mutual consent and for a time, so that you may devote yourselves to prayer. Then come together again so Satan will not tempt you because of your lack of self-control (1 Corinthians 7:5).

It is love that causes a man to put the needs of his wife before his own interests, and vice versa.

Spouses who practice sexual self-gratification are operating from a covetous heart. There should be no room in a Christian marriage for self-seeking sex. Selfish attitudes place personal needs above one's spouse instead of placing the spouse's needs above one's own. Self-seeking husbands and wives are not interested in fulfilling their conjugal rights with their spouse: they are interested in being fulfilled. That is not love; it is greed. Christlike love gives unilaterally without expecting anything in return.[142]

When God has the primacy in a marital relationship, self will be surrendered, and the love of Christ will motivate the spouses. This is of absolute importance if couples are to deny emotion the controlling center of the marriage.

It should always be remembered that the goal of marriage is not "being in love" or sexual fulfillment. The goal is "to be a reflection on the human level of our ultimate love relationship and union with the Lord."[143] This goal motivates couples to work on habits and love one another.

❧❦

Discussion Questions

1. What does the permanence of marriage say about how couples should view romance and the feeling of being in love?

---

[142] John D. Street, *Passions Of The Heart: Biblical Counsel for Stubborn Sexual Sins* (New Jersey: P&R Publishing Company, 2019), 245.

[143] Timothy Keller, *The Meaning of Marriage: Facing the Complexities of Commitment with the Wisdom of God* (New York: Penguin), 226

2. What does it mean to have God first in your physical relationship?
3. How do couples approach the challenge of habit replacement?
4. How does biblical admonition affect how sexuality should be understood in marriage?
5. How do you explain unifying habits, and habit that cause estrangement?
6. What role God plays in our understanding of relationship between husband and wife?
7. Can you think about habits in your marriage that need to be replaced?

CHAPTER ELEVEN

❦

The tryrannous "I don't see how prayer will make a difference."

Prayer is the power by which that comes to pass which otherwise would not take place. —Andrew Murray

Marriage is more than a physical relationship between a man and a woman. For all intents and purposes, it is a permanent spiritual togetherness. Therefore, any neglect of the spiritual could have lasting implications for the condition of the person-to-person commitment. "For our struggle is not against flesh and blood, but against the rulers, against the authorities, against the powers, of the dark world, and against spiritual forces of evil in the heavenly realms (Ephesians 6:12)." Hence, the spiritual dimension of the marriage requires due attention in order to withstand evil spiritual forces, which wage attacks on the very existence of the sacred institution.

Spirituality has to do with the spouses' relationship with God. Deep down within the being of every mate is a longing and desire for God (Ecclesiastes 3:11). God placed that desire there so human beings would transcend the visible and reach out to the Sovereign Creator (Hebrews 11:27). Augustine captures the essence of this reality by writing, "You have made us for yourself, O Lord, and our hearts are restless until they rest in you."[144] While the

---

[144] Augustine, *The Confessions* 1.1, trans. Maria Boulding, *The Works of St. Augustine: A Translation for the Twenty First Century*, ed. John E. Rotelle (Brooklyn, New York: New City Press, 1997),

physical may be admirable, it should lead us to the spiritual connection with God. In the absence that intimacy with God, the marriage is not prepared for spiritual attacks. To spend the time endlessly paying attention to the physical without engaging the spiritual dimension exposes the marriage to the influence of destructive evil forces. Hence Augustine provides helpful counsel in his *Expositions On The Psalms*. He said,

> Learn in the creature to love the Creator; and in the work of Him who made it. Let not that which has been made by Him detain thine affections, so that thou shouldest lose Him by whom thou thyself wert made also… Thou admirest these things because thou seest not Him: but through those things which thou admirest, love Him who thou seest not."[145]

The love for the One not seen moves couples into a relationship that unites them as a solid team against the attacks of Satan. (1 John 4:4, 18–19) While there is so much to admire with the physical, there also exists a lot of disorder in the realm of the visible.

A couple should remember that the marriage exists in a world inundated with disorder, and the Evil One will come to accost the faith of mates (Luke 21:32–33). "On a planet ruled by the Evil One we should expect to see violence, deception, disease and all manner of opposition to the reign of God."[146] Should these come into the marriage, the faith of spouses will be tested. However, when couples move towards God, naturally, the couple gets closer to each other. This is a strong position for spiritual warfare. "The closer we come to Christ, the nearer we shall be to one another."[147] A couple's strongest and most unifying spiritual power in a marriage is prayer. "When your hands are enclosed in prayer, it acknowledges the third party in your relationship, the God who blessed your marriage and continues to sustain your love for each other."[148] Prayer will keep disorder out of marriage by resourcing

---

1/1:139. Cited in Kelly M. Kapic *A Little Book For New Theologians* (Downers Grove, ILL: IVP, 2012), 22.

[145] Quoted in Kenneth Boa, *Conformed To His Image: Biblical and Practical Approaches To Spiritual Formation* (Grand Rapids, MI: Zondervan, 2001), 189.

[146] Philip Yancey, *Prayer: Does It Make Any Difference* (Grand Rapids, MI: Zondervan, 2006), 118.

[147] Ellen G. White, *The Adventist Home*, (Hagerstown, MD: Review and Herald Publishing Association), 179.

mates with Divine power to combat evil forces. Divine power is God's response to prayer (Acts 2:1–5). If there is disorder, prayer will dissipate the confusion. Karl Barth declared, "To clasp the hands in prayer is the beginning of an uprising against the disorder in the world."[149] Similarly, prayer will begin an offensive against any evil attack on your marriage.

The weapon of a couple's warfare

The attempt of Satan is to first weaken faith in God. When faith is weakened, then all cracks in the marriage will be severely exploited. The tools used against personal faith in God are crises (Job 1–3; Ruth 1–2). In the case of Job, his wife's faith appeared to have collapsed under a relentless bout of one crisis after another. The marriage seemed to have been severely damaged. "Regrettably, marriages often pay the price when the strain creates relational conflict. Indeed all of the footholds listed in this section—personal sin, spousal blame, unrighteous anger, marital inattention, and financial worries—can erupt under the weight of a faith struggle."[150] Marriage should prepare for spiritual battles (John 10:10). No couple will live happily ever after. Never look at the misfortune of others and say, "This cannot happen to my marriage." There are battles to fight.

> The battles should not be fought alone. Marriage is not for loners. God's intention is for our spouses to be our allies—intimate friends, lovers, warriors in the spiritual warfare against the forces of the evil One. We are to draw strength, nourishment, and courage to fight well from that one person who most deeply supports and joins us in the war—our soul mate for life. Husbands and wives are intimate allies.[151]

This kind of unbreakable partnership is sustainable when both come together in prayer. Prayer is the weapon of the couple's warfare. It is uniting human capabilities with Divine power (2 Peter 1:3; 2 Corinthians 10:4–5).

---

[148] Alberta Mazart, *The Intimate Marriage: Connecting With The One You Love*, (Hagerstown, MD: 2001), 97.

[149] Philip Yancey *Prayer* 118. He quoted the words of Karl Barth.

[150] William F. Cook III & Chuck Lawless, (Nashville, TN: B&H Publishing, 2019), 304.

[151] Da. B. Allender and Tremper Longman III, *Intimate Allies: Rediscovering God's Design for Marriage and Becoming Soul Mates for Life* (Wheaton, IL: Tyndale House, 1999), xvi.

Couples prayer is not slipshod but disciplined and consistent personal devotion and family worship. Daily worship in the home provides the opportunity to unite in prayer. "The Bible clearly implies that God deserves to be worshiped daily in our homes by our families."[152] In 1 Peter 3:7, the Apostle writes, "Husbands, in the same way be considerate as you live with your wives, and treat them with respect as the weaker partner, and as heirs with you, of the gracious gift of life, so that nothing will hinder your prayers." In the same epistle, he writes, "Be self-controlled and alert. Your enemy the devil prowls around like a roaring lion looking for someone to devour (1 Peter 5:8)." It is expected that married couples will pray together in family worship, and allow nothing to disconnect them from Divine power. The husband is specifically mentioned in 1 Peter 3:7. Husbands have a prominent role and responsibility to protect the prayer partner ministry in the marriage. Any disconnection from God due to relational or marital issues could block the efficacy and efficiency of the prayer (Psalm 66:18). Such spiritual weakness could open the door to the malignant attacks and sophistry of Satan, who prowls around looking for a marriage to devour.

Strategies for use of the weapon of prayer
1. Each spouse should engage in personal daily devotion. This includes prayer and the study of the Bible. The prayer should include praise, thanksgiving, confession of sins and a plea for the righteousness of Christ, an infilling of the Holy Spirit, and wisdom. Ephesians 6:18; Philippians 4:4–7.
2. Every day couples should come together and welcome the Holy Spirit into their lives and the marriage. The prayer should seek for a fresh baptism of the Holy Spirit. Acts 2:38-39.
3. Every day couples should read the promises of God's word to one another and then claim the promises. The prayer should include names of the mates in the scriptural promise. For example, "Then shall <u>Ruth</u> call and the Lord will answer; <u>Ruth</u> shall cry and he shall say, 'Here I am.'" Isaiah 58:9. The promise should be in the context of the mate's life situation.
4. Couples should come together discuss the plans for the day and then, in prayer, put the plans in the hand of God. The prayer should seek

---

[152] Donald S. Whitney, *Family Worship* (Wheaton IL: Crossway, 2016), 27.

God's blessing on the plans according to the will of God. James 4:13-17; Isaiah 46:9–10.

5. Husbands and wives should probe the areas of concerns in their marriage and then put the matter before the Lord in prayer. Rachel said to Jacob, "Give me children or I'll die!" Jacob became angry with her and said, "Am I in the place of God who has kept you from having children?" Genesis 30:1–2. God settled the issue. It is written, "Then God remembered Rachel; he listened to her and opened her womb." Genesis 30:27.

6. List the spiritual responsibilities of each other and then ask God for wisdom and strength to perform the tasks. Sometimes physical matters could displace spiritual responsibilities. When Moses forgot to circumcise his son, Zipporah, his wife, carried out the function. Exodus 4:25. Spiritual responsibility should not be lost in daily grind of other activities.

7. Place hands on each other's heads and bless one another with scriptural promises. For example, "I keep asking that the God of our Lord Jesus Christ, the glorious Father, may give you the Spirit of wisdom and revelation so that you may know him better." Ephesians 1:17 At the same time, pray against idols of the heart (Ezekiel 14:1–11). Samson lost his way because of heart idols.

8. Talk about emotional issues and seek the Lord for wisdom to think correctly. Ruth 1:16-17.

9. Talk about dissatisfaction about any matter and the toll it is taking. Then join in prayer and together seek the Lord for discernment. The story of Elkanah and Hannah could be helpful. 1 Samuel 1.

10. Couples should pray for faith to handle misfortunes in life. Job 1–3.

11. Couples should pray against any tendency to manipulate one another.1 Kings 16:31–33.

12. Mates should pray for a forgiving heart should any mate fall into sin. Hosea 1–3.

13. Couples should take turns in prayer and fasting for one another. Mark 9:14–30.

14. Couples should construct a list of other married couples and pray for them and also request their prayers. Colossians 4:3.

Prayer will definitely make a difference in all areas of the marriage. It is the weapon that takes hold of the Omnipotent hand of God and brings God to bear on situations that threaten the existence of the marriage. This kind of active prayer life will sustain intimate partnership. In fact, it fosters a feeling of togetherness that enrich the marital relationship.

Discussion Questions

1. What kind of crises have you been through in your marriage? How did they turn out? What role did prayer play?
2. How important is family worship in your marriage?
3. What implications your spiritual life has on the marriage?
4. Do you believe that couples should pray together? Why?
5. How can prayer strategy prepare your marriage for spiritual warfare?
6. How do you plan to begin your prayer offensive or strengthen it?

CONCLUSION

❧❧

If I were asked to discuss the most salient component of correct thinking, I'd say faith in God. Thinking from a position of faith allows couples to bring to bear the mind of God on the daily events taking place in their marriage. In the absence of that spiritual resource, mates tend to address events in a manner that that is driven by self-fulfillment. Therefore, instead of the Bible being the personal system of thought which influences daily decisions, couples interpret and make decisions about marital events on the basis of feelings and the prevailing culture.

Faith reaches out to one beyond us. In other words, God has to be taken into account as the most important person in the marriage. The Sovereign God should be relied upon for correct thinking. "A person may be some what successful at modifying outward behavior, but the only real way to glorify the Lord Jesus Christ is to think according to His Word (Romans 12:2)."[153] Thinking according to the Word of God is correct thinking.

The reality is that incorrect thinking has invaded the sacred space of marriage. Evidences are compelling that the **"I's" have it.** Selfish, narcissistic, naturalistic, and even vengeful thoughts have given rise to the **tyrannous "I's."** In any marriage where the tyrannous "I's" reign, the way out is correct thinking. As couples surrender to Christ, and confess sinful thoughts, the Holy Spirit will give them power to exchange selfish and

---

[153] Martha Peace, *The Excellent Wife: A Biblical Perspective* (Bemidji, Minnesota: FOCUS PUBLISHING INC., 2005), 24.

naturalistic thoughts for other-centered and God-ward thoughts (Romans 5:1–5; Philippians 2:1–8).

Correct thinking saves marriage. Correct thinking is possible. "I have been crucified with Christ and I no longer live, but Christ lives in me. The life I live in the body, I live by faith in the Son of God, who loved me and gave himself for me (Galatians 2:20)." Correct thinking is done from a position of faith in God, through Jesus Christ, where the scripture is brought to bear on marriage.